折射集
prisma

照亮存在之遮蔽

由南京大学郑钢基金资助出版

Nanjing Course:
Reading Marx and Engels in the Age of the Anthropocene—
From *German Ideology* to the *Dialectics of Nature*

Bernard Stiegler

当代激进思想家译丛

● 丛书主编 张一兵

南京课程：
在人类纪时代阅读马克思和恩格斯
——从《德意志意识形态》到《自然辩证法》

南京大学出版社

激进思想天空中不屈的天堂鸟

——写在"当代激进思想家译丛"出版之际

张一兵

传说中的天堂鸟有很多版本。辞书上能查到的天堂鸟是鸟也是一种花。据统计,全世界共有40余种天堂鸟花,在巴布亚新几内亚就有30多种。天堂鸟花是一种生有尖尖的利剑的美丽的花。但我更喜欢的传说,还是作为极乐鸟的天堂鸟,天堂鸟在阿拉伯古代传说中是不死之鸟,相传每隔五六百年就会自焚成灰,由灰中获得重生。在自己的内心里,我们在南京大学出版社新近推出的"当代激进思想家译丛"所引介的一批西方激进思想家,正是这种在布尔乔亚世界大获全胜的复杂情势下,仍然坚守在反抗话语生生灭灭不断重生中的学术天堂鸟。

2007年,在我的邀请下,齐泽克第一次成功访问中国。应该说,这也是当代后马克思思潮中的重量级学者第一次在这块东方土地上登场。在南京大学访问的那些天里,除去他的四场学术报告,更多的时间就成了我们相互了解和沟通的过程。一天他突然很正经地对我说:"张教授,在欧洲的最重要的左翼学者中,你还应该关注阿甘本、巴迪欧和朗西埃,他们都是我很好的朋友。"说实话,那也是我第一次听到这些陌生的名字。虽然在2000年,我已经提出"后马克思思潮"这一概念,但还是局限于对国内来说已经比较热的鲍德里亚、德勒兹和后期德里达,当时,齐泽克也就是我最新指认的拉康式的后马克思批判理论的代表。正是由于齐泽克的推荐,促成了2007年南京大学出版社开始购买阿甘本、朗西埃和巴迪欧等人学术论著的版权,这也开辟了我们这一全新的"当代激进思想家译丛"。之所以没有使用"后马克思思潮"这一概念,而是转启"激进思想家"的学术指称,因之我后来开始关注的一些重要批判理论家并非与马克思的学说有过直接或间接的关联,甚至干脆就是否定马克思的,前者如法国的维里利奥、斯蒂格勒,后者如德国的斯洛特戴克等人。激进话语,可涵盖的内容和外延都更有弹性一些。这一新的研究领域已经开始成为国内西方左翼学术思潮研究新的构式前沿。为此,还真应该谢谢齐泽克。

那么,什么是今天的激进思潮呢?用阿甘本自己的指认,激进话语的本质是要做一个"同时代的人"。有趣的是,这个"同时代的人"与我们国内一些人刻意标举的"马克思是我们的同时代的人"的构境意向却正好相反。"同时代就是不合时宜"(巴特语)。不合时宜,即绝不与当下的现实存在同流合污,这种同时代也就是与时代决裂。这表达了一切**激进话语**的本质。为此,阿甘本还专门援引尼采①在1874年出版的《不合时宜的沉思》一书。在这部作品中,尼采自指"这沉思本身就是不合时宜的",他在此书"第二沉思"的开头解释说,"因为它试图将这个时代引以为傲的东西,即这个时代的历史文化,理解为一种疾病、一种无能和一种缺陷,因为我相信,我们都被历史的热病消耗殆尽,我们至少应该意识到这一点"②。将一个时代当下引以为傲的东西视为一种病和缺陷,这需要何等有力的非凡透视感啊!依我之见,这可能也是当代所有激进思想的构序基因。顺着尼采的构境意向,阿甘本主张,一个真正激进的思想家必然会将自己置入一种与当下时代的"断裂和脱节之中"。正是通过这种与常识意识形态的断裂和时代错位,他们才会比其他人更能够感知**乡愁**和把握他们自己时代的本质。③我基本上同意阿甘本的观点。

阿甘本是我所指认的欧洲后马克思思潮中重要的一员大将。在我看来,阿甘本应该算得上近年来欧洲左翼知识群体中哲学功底比较深厚、观念独特的原创性思想家之一。与

---

① 尼采(Friedrich Wilhelm Nietzsche,1844—1900):德国著名哲学家。代表作为《悲剧的诞生》(1872)、《查拉图斯特拉如是说》(1883—1885)、《论道德的谱系》(1887)、《偶像的黄昏》(1889)等。

② Friedrich Nietzsche, "On the Uses and Abuses of History to Life", in *Untimely Meditations*, trans. R. J. Hollingdale, Cambridge: Cambridge University Press, 1997, p. 60.

③ [意]阿甘本:《裸体》,黄晓武译,河南大学出版社2015年版,第7页。

巴迪欧基于数学、齐泽克受到拉康哲学的影响不同,阿甘本曾直接受业于海德格尔,因此铸就了良好的哲学存在论构境功底,加之他后来对本雅明、尼采和福柯等思想大家的深入研读,所以他的激进思想往往是以极为深刻的原创性哲学方法论构序思考为基础的。并且,与朗西埃等人1968年之后简单粗暴的"去马克思化"(杰姆逊语)不同,阿甘本并没有简单地否定马克思,反倒力图将马克思的批判精神与当下的时代精神结合起来,以生成对当代资本主义社会存在更为深刻的批判性透视。他关于"9·11"事件之后的美国"紧急状态"(国土安全法)和收容所现象的一些有分量的政治断言,是令西方资本主义国家政要为之恐慌的天机泄露。这也是我最喜欢他的地方。

朗西埃曾经是阿尔都塞的得意门生。1965年,当身为法国巴黎高师哲学教授的阿尔都塞领着整个西方马克思主义科学思潮向着法国科学认识论和语言结构主义迈进的时候,那个著名的《资本论》研究小组中,朗西埃就是重要成员之一。这一点,也与巴迪欧入世时的学徒身份相近。他们和巴里巴尔、马舍雷等人一样,都是阿尔都塞的名著《读〈资本论〉》(*Lire le Capital*, 1965)一书的共同撰写者。应该说,朗西埃和巴迪欧二人是阿尔都塞后来最有"出息"的学生。然而,他们的显赫成功倒并非因为他们承袭了老师的道统衣钵,反倒是由于他们在1968年"五月风暴"中的反戈一击式的叛逆。其中,朗西埃是在现实革命运动中通过接触劳动者，以完全相反的感性现实回归远离了阿尔都塞。

法国的斯蒂格勒、维里利奥和德国的斯洛特戴克三人都算不上是后马克思思潮的人物，他们天生与马克思主义不亲，甚至在一定的意义上还抱有敌意（比如斯洛特戴克作为当今德国思想界的右翼知识分子，就是反对马克思主义的）。可是，在他们留下的学术论著中，我们不难看到阿甘本所说的那种绝不与自己的时代同流合污的姿态，对于布尔乔亚世界来说，都是"不合时宜的"激进话语。斯蒂格勒继承了自己老师德里达的血统，在技术哲学的实证维度上增加了极强的批判性透视；维里利奥对光速远程在场性的思考几乎就是对现代科学意识形态的宣战；而斯洛特戴克最近的球体学和对资本内爆的论述，也直接成为当代资产阶级全球化的批判者。

应当说，在当下这个物欲横流、尊严倒地，良知与责任在冷酷的功利谋算中碾落成泥的历史时际，我们向国内学界推介的这些激进思想家是一群真正值得我们尊敬的、严肃而有公共良知的知识分子。在当前这个物质已经极度富足丰裕的资本主义现实里，身处资本主义体制之中的他们依然坚执地秉持知识分子的高尚使命，努力透视眼前繁华世界中理直气壮的形式平等背后所深藏的无处控诉的不公和血泪，依然理想化地高举着抗拒全球化资本统治逻辑的大旗，发自肺腑地激情呐喊，振奋人心。无法否认，相对于对手的庞大势力而言，他们显得实在弱小，然而正如传说中美丽的天堂鸟一般,时时处处,他们总是那么不屈不挠。人类社会发展的历史已经明证,内心的理想是这个世界上最无法征服也是力量最大的东西,这种不屈不挠的思考和抗争,常常就是燎原之前照亮人心的点点星火。因此,有他们和我们共在,就有人类更美好的解放希望在!

目 录

引 言 ·········· 001

第一讲　导论:自动化社会的诸多问题(2016年3月21日) ·········· 007

第二讲　在人类纪阅读马克思和海德格尔:自动化社会中的心灵的功能(2016年3月23日) ·········· 039

第三讲　在人类纪阅读马克思和海德格尔:持存、前摄和知识(2016年3月28日) ·········· 065

第四讲　在人类纪阅读马克思和海德格尔:技术中断、人类纪和逆人类纪(2016年3月30日) ·········· 097

第五讲　器官学、经济学和生态学(2016年4月6日) ·········· 131

第六讲　热力学、座架和负人类学(2016年4月9日) ·········· 155

第七讲　器官学的界限和理性的功能(2016年4月11日) ·········· 203

第八讲　在人类纪阅读马克思:从《德意志意识形态》到《资本论》(2016年4月13日) ·········· 267

引 言

I propose the following title and syllabus:

我计划讲授下述课程名称与提纲:

Reading Marx and Engels in the Age of the Anthropocene
From *German Ideology* to the *Dialectics of Nature*
在人类纪时代阅读马克思和恩格斯
——从《德意志意识形态》到《自然辩证法》

This course will be dedicated to an interpretation of Marx's and Engels's philosophy of technics in the light of phenomenological (Husserl and Heidegger), post-phenomenological (Derrida, Simondon), anthropological (Leroi-Gourhan, Merlin Donald) questions, and scientific questions, mainly thermodynamics and biology according to theories of entropy and negentropy (Schrödinger).

这门课程将致力于从技术哲学的角度来阐释马克思和恩格斯的哲学，我们将从现象学（胡塞尔、海德格尔）、后现象学（德里达、西蒙栋①）、人类学（勒鲁瓦-古兰②、梅林·唐纳德③）的问题域及科学的问题域——主要是基于熵与负熵理论的热力学及生物学问题（薛定谔）入手。

The aim of the course is to reconsider the contemporary forms of capitalism in the light of what will be described as a general organology, itself constituting the political question of a "pharmacology" (in the derridean sense of the word "pharmakon"). The Anthropocene is often apprehended as the transformation of anthropogenesis by the capitalist industrial revolution. The process of automation provoked by the digitalization engaged an acceleration that is now named in

---

① 吉尔伯特·西蒙栋（Gilbert Simondon, 1924—1989）：当代法国著名技术哲学家。1958 年在乔治·康吉莱姆的指导下通过博士论文《形式与信息概念中的个体化》（L'individuation à la lumière des notions de formes et d'information）。曾任教于普瓦提埃大学（1960—1963）、巴黎大学人文科学院（1963—1969）、巴黎第五大学（1969—1984），并创建了亨利·皮罗恩（Henri Piéron）"普通心理学和实验技术"研究所。其代表作有：《技术客体的存在方式》（1958）、《心理个体化与集体个体化》（1989）等。——译者注

② 安德烈·勒鲁瓦-古兰（André Leroi-Gourhan, 1911—1986）：法国考古学家、古生物学家、人类学家。曾任法兰西学院教授（1969—1982）、巴黎人类博物馆副馆长。其代表作有：《人与物》（1943）、《手势与言语》（2 卷，1964—1965）等。——译者注

③ 梅林·唐纳德（Merlin Donald, 1939—　）：加拿大心理学家、神经人类学家、认知神经学家。加拿大皇家学会会员。1968 年获加拿大麦吉尔大学神经心理学博士学位。加拿大皇后大学荣誉退休教授、美国凯斯西储大学认知科学系创始主席（2005）。其代表作有：《现代思想的起源：文化和认知演变的三个阶段》（1991）、《如此罕见的心智：人类意识的进化》（2001）等。——译者注

American theory of innovation "disruption" (see Clayton Christensen), and that we will try to consider according to the concepts of Gestell and Ereignis interpreted with the help of Rudolf Boehm's analysis.

  本课程的目的是对资本主义的当代诸形式（contemporary forms）进行重新阐释，这将被描述为一般器官学（general organology），它本身构成了药理学（pharmacology，德里达意义上的法文词为"pharmakon"）的政治问题。人类纪（Anthropocene）经常被解读为由资本主义工业革命所引发的一种人类起源的转型（transformation of anthropogenesis）。由数字化所激发的自动化过程（process of automation provoked by the digitalization）加速了这种转型，这种加速在美国的创新理论（theory of innovation，参见克莱顿·克里斯坦森[①]）中被命名为"中断（disruption）"。我们将基于鲁道夫·勃姆的分析，运用座架（Gestell）和生成（Ereignis）等概念来阐释这一点。

[①] 克莱顿·克里斯坦森（Clayton Christensen, 1953— ）：美国管理学家、创新理论大师。美国哈佛大学商学院教授。其代表作有：《创新者的窘境》（1997）等。——译者注

Bibliography	参考书目
Karl Marx and Friedrich Engels, *The German Ideology*	马克思、恩格斯,《德意志意识形态》
Friedrich Engels, *Dialectics of Nature*	恩格斯,《自然辩证法》
Edmund Husserl, *Origin of Geometry*	胡塞尔,《几何学的起源》
Martin Heidegger, *Time and Being*	海德格尔,《时间与存在》
Martin Heidegger, *Identity and Difference*	海德格尔,《同一与差异》
Rudolf Boehm, *Pensée et technique*	鲁道夫·勃姆,《技术之思》
André Leroi-Gourhan, *Gesture and Speech*	勒鲁瓦-古兰,《手势与言语》
Merlin Donald, *Origin of the Modern Mind*	梅林·唐纳德,《现代思想的起源》
Erwin Schrödinger, *What is Life?*	薛定谔,《生命是什么?》

Each course will be followed by a presentation on one text of the bibliography by two students.

每节课后,每两个学生组成一组,根据书目中的一个文本提供一个研究报告。

Each student will write an essay addressing a theme of the course.

每个学生都要写一篇与课程主题相关的课程论文。

Please tell me what you think about this proposal. I suggest that for examination the presentation counts for 40% and the essay (around 2500 words) for 60%.

请告诉我你的论文概要。我建议在考核中研究报告占40%，论文（约2500字）占60%。

**FIRST COURSE
21 MARCH 2016
/**
Introduction to the Questions of the
Automatic Society

第 一 讲
2016.3.21
导论
自动化社会的诸多问题

During this seminar, we will try to read, think and interpret Marx and Heidegger in the same movement of thinking.

在这次研讨课上，我们将尝试用同一思路对马克思和海德格尔进行阅读、思考和解读。

It is the question of **exosomatisation** that will lead this double reading and questioning—exosomatisation being what one calls more generally **technics**. But thus considered, as exosomatisation, technics appears as a stage of **organogenesis** that the **evolution of life** is. In such a view, technics is not the opposite of life, but its evolution, a continuation of life by other means than life.

我们将以**外在化**（**exosomatisation**）问题来引导这种双重阅读和提问——外在化就是通常所说的**技术**（**technics**）。但需要注意的是，作为外在化的技术，是作为**生命进化**的**器官形成**（**organogenesis**）的一个阶段而出现的。从这个角度来看，技术不是生命的对立面，而是生命的进化，一种借助生命之外的其他手段而实现的生命的延续。

A living being is an **organism**, as it was said by Lamarck, and the evolution of these organisms is an **organogenesis**. Hominisation, which begins between two and three million years ago, is also the beginning of an exosomatisation where **the human body begins to produce exosomatic organs**, that are artificial organs—**non-organic organs**—I call also **organological organs**.

如拉马克（Lamarck）所言，一个生物就是一个**有机体**（**organism**），而这些有机体的进化就是一种**器官形成**（**organogenesis**）。始于两三百万年前的人化过程（Hominisation），也是外在化的开始，即**人的身体开始产生体外器官**（**exosomatic organs**），而体外器官就是人造器官（artificial organs）：**非有机的器官**（**non-organic organs**）。我也称之为**器官学意义上的器官**（**organological organs**）。

This is what is generally called technics. Now, if we agree to say that every thing that is the product of such an exosomatisation, of such an ex-teriorisation, or ex-ternalisation, is technical, then, we must say that **language, as it is a social production, belongs to exosomatisation**, and in this sense, **belongs to technics.**

这就是通常所说的技术。现在，如果我们同意任何事物作为这种外在化（exosomatisation）、外化（ex-teriorisation）或客观化（ex-ternalisation）的产物都是技术性的，那么我们就必须说，因为**语言是一种社会生产，所以它属于外在化**。从这个意义上说，**语言也属于技术**（technics）。

Technics is what I try to think with the concepts of what I call:

1. **general organology** and
2. **pharmacology.**

而我试图用我称之为**一般器官学**（**general organology**）和**药理学**（**pharmacology**）的一些概念来思考技术。

*

As a stage of evolution, as the pursuit of the organogenesis, and, in this sense, as the continuation of the life—an **organisation** of matter as **organic matter**—by an organisation of matter as **organised inorganic matter**, technics necessarily belongs to this process that is called, since Erwin Schrödinger, the **negative entropy**, or **negentropy**. Now,

1. to think negentropy, we must first understand **what is entropy**.

2. We must check whether **organised inorganic matter opens the possibility of something that is different from entropy as well as negentropy.**

作为进化的一个阶段，作为器官形成的目标，在这个意义上，也作为借助**有序的无机物（organised inorganic matter）组织**而实现的生命——一种**有机物（organic matter）组织**——的延续，技术必然属于这样一个过程，即自从埃尔温·薛定谔（Erwin Schrödinger）① 以来就被称为**否定的熵（negative entropy）**或**负熵（negentropy）**的过程。现在，

1. 为了说明负熵，我们必须首先理解**什么是熵（entropy）**；

2. 我们必须考察一下<u>有序的无机物</u>组织**是否打开了某种不同于熵和负熵的东西的可能性**。

Here it is very important to notice that, **contrary to Heidegger, Marx couldn't know the concept of <u>negentropy</u>.** Now, even if **Engels will talk about entropy in his *Dialectics of nature*, he will not really take its novelty into account.** As to Heidegger, Heidegger will **never consider entropy and negentropy** in his thought of **being and becoming.**

这里值得注意的是，**相对于海德格尔，马克思不可能知道<u>负熵</u>概念**。即使**恩格斯在《自然辩证法》中谈到熵，他也不会想到它的新内涵**。至于**海德格尔**，他绝不会在关于**存在（being）**与**生成（becoming）**的思想中考虑到熵和

---

① 埃尔温·薛定谔（Erwin Schrödinger, 1887—1961）：奥地利物理学家、量子力学奠基人之一。曾获诺贝尔物理学奖（1933）、马克斯·普朗克奖章（1937）。苏黎世大学、柏林大学和格拉茨大学教授。其代表作有：《波动力学四讲》（1928/1952）、《生命是什么？——活细胞的物理面貌》（1946）等。——译者注

负熵。

The goal of this seminar is **to rethink political economy, a new critic of political economy, in the context of what one calls the Anthropocene—a huge and fast increasing of the rate of entropy in the biosphere**—and in the **perspective of what I will call the Neganthropocene.**

这次研讨课的目的是**重新思考政治经济学**，即一种从所谓的人类纪（Anthropocene）——它是**生物圈中熵率的巨大而迅速的增长**——的语境和我所说的逆人类纪（Neganthropocene）的角度而展开的新政治经济学批判。

The goal is to reach such a concept through **a new reading of Marx and Heidegger under the light of the questions opened by entropy and negentropy** in the sphere of the **exosomatic form of life** that is ours—as humankind living on the earth and in the era of Anthropocene, that is, also, in the disruption, which is the age of the concretisation of Heidegger called the *Gestell*.

我们的目标就是**在由熵与负熵在我们的外在化的生命形式领域中所打开的问题域下，通过重新阅读马克思和海

德格尔来达到这一概念——而我们外在化的生命形式就是我们生活在地球上的人类在人类纪时代，亦即在海德格尔所说的*座架*（*Gestell*）的具体化时代的中断之中［所经历的存在形式］。

*

Anthropocene is a geological era, that appeared two hundred and fifty years ago, with industrialisation and capitalism, this being also a new stage in the history of exosomatisation.

I will try to show you **why and how this era can and must be overcome.**

人类纪是一种地质学新纪元，已有 250 年的历史。随着工业化和资本主义的发展，这种存在也进入外在化历史的新阶段。

我将尝试说明，这个新纪元为什么和怎样能够被克服而且必须被克服。

As a **huge, systemic and extremely fast process of increasing of entropy**, the Anthropocene necessarily leads to **the destruction of all kind of life**, and first, of the human life. Besides, as the **digital disruption** that is currently destroying all kinds of social systems, in the sense of Bertrand Gille and Niklas Luhmann, replacing them by **technologies of hypercontrol**, that is called **algorithmic governmentality**, the end of the Anthropocene is also the attempt to impose a **new ideology**, that is called **transhumanism**.

作为一个巨大的、系统的和极其快速的熵的增长过程，人类纪必然会导致所有生命的毁灭，而人类生命则首当其冲。此外，作为正在破坏一切社会系统的**数字化中断**（the **digital disruption**），即贝特兰·吉尔（Bertrand Gille）① 和尼克拉斯·卢曼（Niklas Luhmann）② 意义上的用**超级控制技术**（technologies of hypercontrol）（即所谓的**算法治理术**［algorithmic governmentality］）取代社会系统，人类纪的目的也是试图推行一种**新的意识形态**，即**超人类主义**（**transhumanism**）。

Transhumanism is a discourse concerning a **new stage of exosomatisation**, that is also **a new kind of endosomatisation**,

---

① 贝特兰·吉尔（Bertrand Gille, 1920—1980）：法国技术史学家。提出技术系统理论，曾任法国巴黎第一大学教授。其代表作有：《技术史》（1978）等。——译者注
② 尼克拉斯·卢曼（Niklas Luhmann, 1927—1998）：当代德国著名社会学家、社会系统论的创新者。其代表作有：《社会系统》（1984）、《社会的社会》（1998）等。——译者注

using for example **neurotechnologies** for **transforming the interior of the brain from the exterior**—I will come back to this topic later. Transhumanism is not only an ideology, but also **a new kind of marketing**, that has its **own university**, called the university of the Singularity, that want to make the market the unique source of criteria for this evolution that exosomatisation is.

超人类主义是一种关于**新的外在化阶段**的话语，这种新的外在化阶段也是一种**新的内在化**（endosomatisation），比如利用**神经技术从外部转化到大脑的内部**——后面我会回到这个话题。超人类主义不仅是一种意识形态，也是一**种新的市场营销**（marketing），它有自己的大学，即奇点大学（the university of Singularity），它想使市场成为外在化即进化的唯一标准来源。

Overcoming the Anthropocene is to oppose to such an ideology, to such a marketing, and then to such a market of exosomatisation, **a revolutionary movement in economy**, that I call **the advent of Neganthropocene**.

克服人类纪就要反对这种意识形态，反对这种市场营销，进而实现这样一种外在化的市场和**经济革命运动**，我称之为**逆人类纪的到来**(the advent of Neganthropocene)。

And I will try to show you that it is possible and necessary to interpret Heidegger's concepts of *Gestell* and *Ereignis* as **exosomatization in the Anthropocene and *Ereignis* as Neganthropocene.**

我认为,这样一种解读是可能和必要的,**即把海德格尔的*座架*(*Gestell*)和*生成*(*Ereignis*)概念理解为人类纪意义上的外在化,将*生成*理解为逆人类纪。**

Neganthropocene is **a new understanding of what is economy.** In such an economy, the primordial value is **negentropy**—the **organisation** as it is **based on the increasing of diversity-biodiversity** as well as **no diversity**, that is, **as knowledge. Knowledge is indeed, at least, negentropic.** But we will see that we could say that knowledge is **neguanthropic** and not only **neguentropic.**

逆人类纪是一种对经济的新理解。在这种经济中,原始价值(primordial value)是**负熵**,也就是说,**组织既建立在多样性-生物多样性不断增长的基础之上,也建立在非多样性,比如知识的不断增长的基础之上。知识的确至少**

是负熵的（negentropic）。但是，我们可能还可以说，知识不仅是负熵的，而且是负人类的（neguanthropic）。

*

Marx and Engels were **the first thinkers of exosomatisation**, this is what is described in ***The German Ideology***, and we of course will go back to this text in the next courses. Now, **exosomatisation, as a continuation of the organogenesis, that is of life, and then, of neguentropy, is not <u>organic</u>, but <u>organologic</u>**, and this means that the artificial organs that are produced by and as exosomatisation are <u>both negentropic *and* entropic.</u>

马克思和恩格斯是**提出外在化的第一代思想家**：这就涉及他们在《德意志意识形态》中所论述的内容，我们将在下一次课上回到这个文本。现在我们要说的是，**作为一种器官形成的延续，作为一种生命的延续和负熵的延续，外在化不是<u>器官的</u>（*organic*），而是<u>器官学的</u>（*organologic*）**，这意味着由外在化产生、并作为外在化的人造器官（artificial organs），<u>既是负熵的（negentropic），又是熵的（entropic）</u>。

This **double-sided structure** of the exosomatic organs means that **these organs are *pharmaka*** , as it is said in ancient Greece by Socrates. And here appear to us **two questions**.

How is it possible to reinterpret Marx,

1. under the light of **negentropy—even as neguanthropy— that is the exosomatisation**?

2. as the **pharmacological question** posed by the double-sided of **artificial organs as they are also entropic**—and that is sometimes also called anthropisation?

体外器官（exosomatic organs）的**双重结构（double-sided structure）**意味着，**这些器官就是**古希腊苏格拉底所说的**药（*pharmaka*）**。这就带来了**两个问题**：

1. 从**负熵**——正如**负人类（neguanthropy）**——即**外在化**的角度重新诠释马克思何以可能？

2. 正如**人造器官也是熵的**一样——有时它也被称为人类活动（anthropisation），从**人造器官**的两面性所引出的**药理学问题（pharmacological question）**角度，重新诠释马克思何以可能？

We will go to the **chapter on machines and automation** in the *Grundrisse* to situate those questions in our context of **integral and generalized automation** that is currently rising. And

I will talk now about this context, in order to introduce the historical and *geschichtlich* situation in which we must **read Marx today.**

All of this will lead us to **read Heidegger in a new light.**

我们将结合今天正在发展着的、**不可或缺的和普遍的自动化的语境**，回到《**大纲**》①中关于机器和自动化（automation）的章节来探讨这些问题。现在，我就来谈一下这种语境，介绍一下这种历史学的（historical）和具有*历史性的*（*geschichtlich*）境况，在这种境况中，我们今天必须**阅读马克思**。

所有这些都将引导我们**从新的角度来阅读海德格尔**。

*

Hurrying at the last moment to finish the preparations for this seminar, I have decided to slightly rearrange its schedule—to be specific, I have decided to change the order of the opening sessions, and to begin with a description of the main features of the context within which I propose the topics that will here be addressed—with the aim of

---

① 斯蒂格勒这里的《大纲》即马克思的《1857—1858 年经济学手稿》，在西方学术界通常称为"大纲"(*Grundrisse*)。下同。——译者注

introducing my audience to a specific proposal: **to undertake the transdisciplinary work that is required as a result of those technological mutations brought about by the Anthropocene, the industrial revolution, and capitalism.**

我之前在准备这次研讨课时，就决定稍微改变一下它的课程安排——具体来说，我觉得改变一下开场讲座（opening sessions）的顺序，即首先概述讲座语境的主要特点，并提出我们要讨论的话题——其目的是向我的听众提一个特别的建议：**从事跨学科研究（transdisciplinary work），这是由作为人类纪、工业革命和资本主义所带来的技术突变（technological mutation）所提出的要求。**

This proposal is for what I call a **general organology**, itself understood as **a theoretical platform specifying the terms of an agreement between the disciplines in every field of knowledge**. This platform defines the **rules for analysing, thinking and prescribing human facts at three parallel but indissociable levels**:

 1. the **psychosomatic**, which is the <u>endosomatic</u> level of **organic organs**;

 2. the **artifactual**, which is the <u>exosomatic</u> level of **organological organs**;

3. the **social**, which is the **organisational** level of **institutional organisms** or of **corporations**.

这个建议是为了便于理解我所说的**一般器官学**（**general organology**）。它本身被理解为这样一种理论平台，即用来具体说明在每一知识场（**field of knowledge**）的不同学科之间的可通约的各种术语。这个平台从三个平行的、但不可分离的层面界定了分析、思考和规定人类事实的规则，这三个层面是：

1. **心理的**（**psychosomatic**）层面，即有机器官的**体内的**（**endosomatic**）层面；

2. **人造的**（**artifactual**）层面，即**器官学意义上的器官**的**体外的**（**exosomatic**）层面；

3. **社会的**（**social**）层面，即机构组织或团体的**组织性的**（**organisational**）层面。

Hence this involves an analysis of the **relations** between **organic organs, technical organs and social organizations**—given that our point of departure consists in the claim that **a human psychosomatic organ always exists in a relationship with artificial organs**, and that **this relationship is always prescribed by social organisations, where the latter are themselves overdetermined by those same artificial organs and their** arrangement with human psychosomatic organs.

因此，这就包含了对**有机器官、技术器官（technical organs）**和社会组织之间的关系的分析——实际上，我们的出发点内含着这样一种观点：**人类的心理器官总是与人造器官相联系而存在，而这种联系又总是被社会组织所规定着，同时社会组织本身又被同一人造器官及其与人类心理器官的安排所过度决定着。**

I must add here—and I will of course develop this in the coming sessions—that **it is always possible for the arrangements between these psychosomatic and artifactual organs to become toxic and destructive** for the organic organs, and hence also for the body within which they dwell. In other words, **a general organology is a pharmacology.**

这里，我必须补充一下——当然，我会在接下来的课中做进一步说明——**这样一种情况总是有可能的，即心理器官和人造器官之间的安排**会变得对有机器官，进而对有机器官所栖居的身体（body）**产生毒性（toxic）和破坏性（destructive）**。也就是说，**一般器官学就是一种药理学**。

This having been said, and before explaining these

points any further, let's engage ourselves with a specification of **our current context**, as humans who belong to an era that since Crutzen has been referred to as the **Anthropocene**.

前面已经说过，在做进一步解释之前，让我们对**我们现在的[时代]语境**做一个说明。这是人类所从属的一个新纪元，它从克鲁岑（Crutzen）① 开始就被指认为**人类纪**。

*

I argued ten years ago that we have entered the **hyper-industrial age**, that ours is an epoch of great **symbolic misery**, and that this leads to the **structural destruction of desire**, that is, it **ruins** the **libidinal economy—speculative marketing**, having become hegemonic, systematically exploits the drives, which are **divested of every attachment**.

我认为，十年前我们就已经进入了**超级工业时代**（hyper-industrial age），这是一个严重**象征性贫困**（great symbolic misery）的纪元。它导致**欲望的结构性毁灭**

---

① 保罗·约瑟夫·克鲁岑（Paul Jozef Crutzen, 1933— ）：荷兰大气化学家、诺贝尔化学奖得主（1995）。自 2000 年首次提出"人类纪"概念以来，该思想已对地质学、环境科学、人类学以及技术哲学等众多领域产生广泛影响。其代表作有：《人类纪》（2000）、《人类地质学》（2002）等。——译者注

(structural destruction of desire），也就是说，它摧毁了力比多经济（libidinal economy），即**投机的市场营销**，而已经变得具有霸权性，并系统性地利用各种驱力（drives），而这些驱力的一切附属物都被剥夺了。

Symbolic misery derives from what, with Nicolas Donin, we call the **mechanical turn of sensibility**, that is an organological change, which places the sensory life of the individual under the permanent control of the mass media.

象征性贫困源于所谓的**感性的机械转向（mechanical turn of sensibility）**（尼古拉斯·杜宁［Nicolas Donin］有着同样的说法），这是一种器官学意义上的变化，即把个人的感性生活置于大众传媒的永恒控制之下。

The causes of symbolic misery and the destruction of desire are **both economic and organological**—it is a matter both of the **consumerist model**, and of those **instruments that capture and harness consumer attention**, implemented by the culture industries and the mass media at the beginning of the twentieth century. These instruments, controlled by marketing, **bypass and short-circuit the savoir-vivre of consumers, their knowledge of how to live.**

象征性贫困的原因和欲望的毁灭**既是经济学的，也是器官学的**：它既与那种**消费主义模式**有关，也与 20 世纪初期借助文化工业和大众传媒来**俘获和控制消费者的注意力**的各种工具有关。这些由市场营销控制的工具**绕过消费者关于如何生活的知识（savoir-vivre）**，使他们在这些方面发生短路。

Consumers are thereby **proletarianized**, just as producers had been proletarianized in the nineteenth century by instruments that short-circuited their savoir-faire, their knowledge of how to make and do, this being fully accomplished at the beginning of the twentieth century.

由此，消费者就**被无产阶级化**了，正如 19 世纪的生产者被使关于如何做的知识（savoir-faire）发生短路的工具所无产阶级化一样，后者在 20 世纪早期就被彻底完成了。

In production as well as in consumption, this industrial capture of attention also **deforms** this attention.

1. Attention is **formed** through **education**, *via* processes of **identification** (in the sense of Freud, that is, as primary and secondary identifications), an education which constitutes **intergenerational relations at the core of which the**

knowledge of how to live is elaborated.

2. To **raise a child** is to **singularly transmit a savoir-vivre**, which they will singularly transmit in their turn—to his or her comrades, friends, family and peers, both near and distant.

3. **What is formed** through all the pathways of education—including teaching—**is that which the industrial capture of attention systematically de-forms**.

在生产和消费中，这种工业性的捕获注意力也**改变了**这种注意力：

1. 注意力是通过**教育**，通过**认同（identification**，这是在弗洛伊德意义上而言的第一认同和第二认同）过程而**塑造的**，关于如何生活的知识占据着代际关系的核心，而构成这种代际关系的教育是精致而复杂的；

2. **养育子女就是以独特的方式传递一种关于如何生活的知识**，然后子女会接着将这种教育以独特的方式传递给他或她的伙伴、朋友、家庭以及无论远近的同辈人；

3. 通过教育的一切途径——包括教学——所**塑造**的东西正是**工业性的捕获注意力**所**系统性地改变（de-form）**的东西。

The economy of desire is formed through processes of

identification and transindividuation, woven in the course of intergenerational relations as the set of capacities **to bind the drives by diverting their aims towards social investments.** The industrial **deformation and diversion** of attention **short-circuits and bypasses** these processes of identification and transindividuation. As such, **the symbolic misery imposed by consumer capitalism, which amounts to de-symbolization,** leads *inevitably* to the destruction of the libidinal economy.

欲望经济是通过认同和超个体化（transindividuation）的过程而形成的，并与作为通过转移驱力的社会投资目标来约束驱力的诸多能力的代际关系相互交织着。注意力的工业性变形和转移绕过了这些认同和超个体化的过程，并使它们发生短路。这样一来，由去符号化（de-symbolization）的消费者资本主义（consumer capitalism）导致的象征性贫困就不可避免地导致力比多经济的毁灭（destruction of the libidinal economy）。

During the second half of the twentieth century, there was a continual decrease of the age at which attention was captured in an industrial way: in the **sixties,** *juvenile* "available brain time" constituted the **prime** target of the audiovisual mass media, but by the end of the century, it was *infantile*

brain time that was being targeted and diverted from its affective and social environment, via all manner of programs and specialized channels—like "Baby First", a channel belonging to Fox TV.

在 20 世纪下半叶，这个以工业方式捕获注意力的<u>时代发生持续衰落</u>：在 **60** 年代，*未成年人的*"可用大脑时间（**available brain time**）"成为视听大众传媒的**首要目标**。但是到了 20 世纪末，通过各种节目和特别频道——比如"宝贝第一（Baby First）"这档属于福克斯电视台（Fox TV）的频道，**婴幼儿的大脑时间**（*infantile* **brain time**）被从情感环境和社会环境中转移出来而成为［大众传媒的新的］目标。

*

The object of desire is *desired* to the point of inverting the goals of the drives that support it, but this is so only because it **does** *more than just exist*: it *consists*, and as such, it *infinitizes itself*, that is, it *exceeds all calculation*. To desire is to **invest** in an object, and to **experience its consistence**, and hence, **to destroy desire is to liquidate all attachment and all fidelity, that is, all confidence**—without which no economy is possible—and ultimately, it is to liquidate *all belief*, and therefore, all *credit*.

欲望的对象渴望能够颠覆支撑它的驱力的诸目标。但是它能够做到这一点，只是因为它**不仅仅是*存在*着：它*构*成了自身，因此它不限制自身，即它*超越了一切计算*。欲望就是投入对象之中，体验它的一致性，因此，消灭欲望就是清除一切依恋（attachment）和一切忠诚（fidelity），即一切信任**——没有这些，任何经济都是不可能的——从而最终清除一切*信仰*（*belief*）和一切*信用*（*credit*）。

The object of desire gives rise to **a spontaneous belief in life that presents itself through this object as its *extra-ordinary* power.** All **love** is **phantasmal** in the sense that **it gives life to that which is not**—to that which is **ordinarily** not. But because **the fantasy of love**, and of what Abdelkebir Khatibi called "aimance" (translated in English as "lovence"), is that which **grants to civilizations their most durable forms**, the literally *fantastic* sentiment in which love *consists* is the incarnation of **a knowledge of the *extra-ordinariness of life* that constantly *surpasses* life**—whereby **life *invents* by going *beyond* life**, and **as the pursuit of life by means other than life**, through the incessant and ever-increasing profusion and evolution of **artifices**.

欲望的对象产生一种生命的自发的信仰，这种信仰通过这个具有<u>超凡（*extra-ordinary*）</u>力量的对象来展现自身。在爱能够赋予那些没有生命的东西——<u>通常没有生命的</u>——以生命的意义上，所有的爱都是幻想性的（**phantasmal**）。但是，因为**这种爱的幻想**，这种阿卜杜勒-卡比尔·哈提比（Abdelkebir Khatibi）所说的"aimance"（译为英文就是"爱之为爱［lovence］"）的幻想**使文明获得最持久的形式**，所以那种真实美妙的爱的感情就成为一种*生命不断超越自身的超凡性知识*的化身——由此，*生命通过超越生命而创造着*，就像生命**借助生命之外的途径**，通过持续的、不断增长的**手段**的进化与丰富而追求着。

This is how I have interpreted the movement of **exteriorisation**—of **exosomatisation**—described by the anthropologist André Leroi-Gourhan in order to analyse the process of hominization as **an invention of life by means other than life**—as <u>**a technological, organological and pharmacological evolution that constitutes the human problem of life on earth**</u>, and the responsibility that we have not to evade this problem, which is constantly being remade by technical invention.

这就是我对人类学家安德烈·勒鲁瓦-古兰所描述的**外化即外在化**运动的解读，目的是分析**通过生命之外的途径进行生命创造**的人化过程——**作为一种工艺学的、器官学的和药理学的进化，它构成了地球上人类的生命难题**。我们无权逃避这一难题，而这一难题将不断被技术发明再生产出来。

Love, as we all know, **is** strictly speaking **the experience of artifice**. It is essential to **fetishize** the one we love, and when we *stop* loving them, we are confronted with the artificiality of the amorous situation, as we are **brought brutally back to the ordinariness of quotidian life.**

我们知道，严格地说，**爱是一种技巧经验（the experience of artifice）**。它对于**迷恋我们所爱之物**是至关重要的，**当我们*停止*爱它们时，我们就会看到这种爱恋情境的人造性质（artificiality），正如我们被残忍地带回到日常生活的平庸（ordinariness）之中。**

Two or three million years ago, life began to pass through the non-living artifice—there first appears what Aristotle referred to as the **noetic soul**, that is, **the soul that loves (as we learn from Diotima in Plato's *Symposium*).**

两三百万年前，生命开始穿越非生命的技巧——第一次出现亚里士多德所说的**智性灵魂**（noetic soul），即**爱的灵魂**（正如我们从柏拉图《会饮篇》中的狄奥提玛那里所学到的一样）。

The non-living artifice **conserves** *for* **life a trace** of what, in the biological economy that Simondon called *vital individuation*, would previously have been lost forever in death. The ***inventive power*** of life that amazed Gilles Clément thus becomes what Paul Valéry described as **the *life of the mind* (*or spirit*)** —which, with modernity and capitalism itself, becomes the ***political economy*** **of spirit,** founded on **industrial technology** that has today become **essential to an *industry of traces*.**

这种非生命的技巧（the non-living artifice）**为生命保存了**一种西蒙栋在生物经济学（biological economy）意义上所说的*生命个体化*（*vital individuation*）的**踪迹**（**trace**），以前这种生命个体化会在死亡中永远消失。后来，令吉尔斯·克莱门特（Gilles Clément）① 惊讶的**生命的*创造力***

---

① 吉尔斯·克莱门特（Gilles Clément, 1943— ）：法国园艺师、景观设计师、植物学家和昆虫学家。1998 年获得法国国家景观奖。——译者注

(*inventive power of life*)成为保罗·瓦莱里(Paul Valéry)①所描述的**思想**(**或精神**)**的生命**(the *life of the mind* [*or spirit*])——随着现代性和资本主义自身的发展,它也变成**精神的政治经济学**(*political economy* of spirit),这种精神的政治经济学建立于**工业技术**(industrial technology),而后者现在对**踪迹工业**来说已变得至关重要(essential to an *industry of traces*)。

The proletarianization of consumers, their de-symbolization, their dis-identification and their confinement within drive-based misery, **subjects all singularities to the calculability** that turns the contemporary world into a desert in which one feels, paradoxically and increasingly, that **as industry innovates more and more**, it somehow turns out that **life is being invented less and less**—a situation that takes to the extreme what Paul Valéry described in 1939 as **the fall in "spirit value."**

消费者的无产阶级化、去符号化、非认同化以及痛苦的分娩使一切独特性都屈从于可计算性。而可计算性使当

---

① 保罗·瓦莱里(Paul Valéry, 1871—1945):法国诗人、散文家、哲学家。法兰西学院院士。其代表作有:《旧诗稿》(1890—1900)、《年轻的命运女神》(1917)等。——译者注

今世界变成一片荒漠，置身其中会荒谬而日益强烈地感到，**随着工业创造得越来越多，结果却是生活被创造得越来越少**——这种境况发展到极点就是保罗·瓦莱里在1939年所描述的"精神价值"的陨落（the fall in "spirit value"）。

The decline of the state, and the **hegemony of strategic marketing and financialization**, were imposed throughout the entire world, and in every part of society, beginning in the nineteen eighties. Along with these changes came **drive-based misery** and **disinvestment**, ruining desire and introducing forms of **disbelief, miscreance and discredit** that continue to afflict **every form of authority, every institution and every business**, eventually leading to the **insolvency** that the collapse of 2008 exposed for all to see.

从20世纪80年代开始，国家的衰落、**战略性的市场营销和金融化的霸权**（hegemony of strategic marketing and financialization）被推行到世界和社会的每一个角落。紧随这些变化而来的是**基于驱力的痛苦**（drive-based misery）和**投资缩减**，并毁灭欲望，产生各种形式的怀疑、异教信仰和信用缺失，它们一直困扰着**每一种权力形式、机构和商业**，最终导致**破产**（insolvency），这就是我们都看到的2008年爆发的大崩溃。

The current and much more recent hegemony of the **industry of traces** tries **to take control of the drives**, through **automation and automatisms founded on social networks**. The drives are, however, ultimately **uncontrollable**, and hence to try and channel the drives in this way, by **mathematical algorithms** to exert an **automated form of social control**, will in the end do nothing but **carry the drives to an extremely dangerous level**, by *dis-integrating* them, turning them into what Felix Guattari and Gilles Deleuze called "dividuals" —and I will go back to this topic later.

当前和最近的**踪迹工业**（**industry of traces**）试图通过基于社会网络建立的自动化（**automation**）和自动主义（**automatism**）控制驱力（**drives**）。然而，驱力归根到底是**不可控制的**（**uncontrollable**），因此又试图通过这样一种方式来引导驱力，即通过**数学算法**（**mathematical algorithms**）来运行一种自动化的社会控制形式。但这最终将无济于事，却将驱力带向极其危险的境地，即通过*分化*（*dis-integrating*）它们而使其变成菲利克斯·瓜塔里和吉尔·德勒兹所说的"分割体（**dividuals**）"。之后我可能会回到这个话题。

**SECOND COURSE
23 MARCH 2016**
/
Reading Marx and Heidegger
in the Anthropocene
The Functions of Mind in the Automatic Society

第 二 讲
2016.3.23
在人类纪阅读马克思和海德格尔:
自动化社会中的心灵的功能

With the advent of **reticular reading and writing**, via globally accessible networks that use those web technologies that began to be implemented around 1993, **digital technologies have led hyper-industrial societies towards a *new stage of proletarianization*.** In this new stage, the hyper-industrial age turned into an era of **systemic stupidity.**

随着通过利用 1993 年左右开始出现的网络技术所搭建的全球性网络而实现的**交互阅读和书写**（reticular reading and writing）的出现，**数字化技术**（digital technologies）已经推动超级工业社会（hyper-industrial societies）进入**无产阶级化的新阶段**。在这个新阶段中，超级工业时代进入一个**系统性愚昧**（systemic stupidity）的时代。

Across networks of **tele-action** (and *tele-objectivity*), production centres can be de-localized, huge markets can be formed, and then remotely controlled, industrial capitalism and financial capitalism can be structurally separated, electronic financial markets can be continuously interconnected, directing in real time the automatisms that are derived from the application of mathematics to the "finance industry." *Processes of automated decisionmaking* can then be **functionally tied to the** *drive-based automatisms* that control **consumer markets**—initially through the mediation of the **mass media**, and, today, **through the industry of traces that is also known as the data economy** (that is, the **economy of *personal data***).

利用*远程-作用*（tele-action）（和*远程-客体性*[*tele-objectivity*]）所织成的网络，生产中心被去地域化，巨大市场被塑造出来，并被远程控制，工业资本主义和金融资本主义被结构性地分离开来，电子金融市场被连续地相互联系起来，实时指挥着数学应用于"金融业"所产生的自动主义。这样一来，*自动决策*(*automated decisionmaking*)*过程就功能性地与基于驱力的自动主义*（*drive-based automatisms*）联系在一起，这种自动主义控制着消费者市场——最初是通过大众传媒的中介，今天则是**通过踪迹工业，亦即数据经济**（the data economy）（即*个人数据经济*

[economy of *personal data*]）的中介而实现的。

Digital automata have succeeded in **bypassing the deliberative functions of the mind**, and a systemic stupidity has been established between consumers and speculators, *functionally based in the drives*, and pitting each against the other—this goes well beyond what Mats Alvesson and André Spicer have called **"functional stupidity"**.

数字化自动装置已经成功**绕过心灵的协商功能**（the deliberative functions of the mind），系统性愚昧已经在消费者和投机商之间*由驱力功能性地*建构起来，使两者相互对立——这已经超出了马茨·阿尔维森（Mats Alvesson）[①]和安德烈·斯派塞（André Spicer）[②]所说的"**功能性愚昧**（functional stupidity）"。

In the last few years, however, and **specifically after 2008**, a state of *generalized stupefaction* seems to have arisen that accompanies this systemic *bêtise*, this functional stupidity.

[①] 马茨·阿尔维森（Mats Alvesson, 1956— ）：瑞典隆德大学经济管理学院教授，以批判管理学研究见长。其代表作有：《愚昧悖论：工作中功能性愚昧的力量与陷阱》（2016）、《批判性管理研究》（2000）等。——译者注

[②] 安德烈·斯派塞（André Spicer）：伦敦城市大学卡斯商学院组织行为学教授，主要从事商业伦理、组织文化、批判管理学等研究。其代表作有：《愚昧悖论：工作中功能性愚昧的力量与陷阱》（2016）等。——译者注

然而,最近几年,尤其是 2008 年之后,**_普遍性麻木_**(*generalized stupefaction*) 状态似乎已经伴随着系统性愚昧(systemic *bêtise*)、功能性愚昧而出现了。

The resulting **stupor** is caused by the most recent *series of technological shocks* that emerged from the digital turn of 1993, that is, with the web—and not only with the internet. The revelation of these shocks, and of their major features and consequences, has brought about a state that is almost literally that of **being stunned**—in particular in the **face of the "four horsemen of the Apocalypse"** (Google, Apple, Facebook and Amazon), and *who appear literally to be <u>disintegrating those industrial societies</u>* that emerged from the *Aufklärung*.

这种正在发生的呆滞(stupor)是由最近**_一系列的技术休克_**(*technological shocks*)引起的,这种技术休克开始于 1993 年的数字化转向,即利用网络——不只是因特网——而引起的数字化转向。这些休克及其主要特点与结果的披露已经产生一种近乎真实的**_震惊状态_**——特别是面对"天启四骑士(four horsemen of the Apocalypse)"(谷歌、苹果公司、脸书和亚马逊),**_它们<u>看起来正在瓦解那些自启蒙</u>(the Aufklärung)<u>以来的工业社会</u>_**。

One result has been what, at a public meeting of Ars Industrialis in Paris, we have referred to as "**net blues**", **suffered by those who had believed or do believe in the promises of the digital era** (including my friends at Ars Industrialis and myself).

其中一个结果就是，在巴黎"精神技术工业政治国际联合会（Ars Industrialis）"的一次公众会议上，**那些相信或信奉数字时代的承诺的人们**（包括我自己和我在联合会的朋友们）都遭遇了我们所说的"网络蓝调（net blues）"①。

*

The hyper-industrial societies that have grown out of the ruins of the industrial democracies constitute **the third stage**

---

① 斯蒂格勒使用"网络蓝调（net blues, *le blues du Net*）"这一概念是为了指认在数字化时代中网络技术的药理学特质。斯蒂格勒指出，过去二十多年里，数字化革命已经利用网络技术对人类生活的各个方面实现了普遍形式化，这在极大改变人们的生活方式和思想观念的同时，也隐藏着巨大的潜在威胁。尤其是2013年爆出的"斯诺登事件"，彻底暴露了网络巨头和黑客分子对私人数据和个人隐私的安全威胁，人们的一切网络行为都被置于赤裸状态，从而引发了人们对网络技术本身的忧虑和质疑。而这正是斯蒂格勒意在表明的网络技术在药理学意义上的毒性效应。对于这一概念的具体阐释，请参见斯蒂格勒于2013年9月所做的专题讲座实录：http://reseaux.blog.lemonde.fr/2013/09/29/blues-net-bernard-stiegler/（法文版）和http://www.samkinsley.com/2013/11/21/bernard-stiegler-the-net-blues/（英文版）。——译者注

of completed proletarianization: in the nineteenth century, we saw the loss of savoir-faire, and the loss of savoir-vivre in the twentieth. **In the twenty-first century, we are witnessing the dawn of the age of the loss of *savoirs théoriques*, of theoretical knowledge** —as if the cause of our being stunned was an *absolutely unthinkable development*.

从工业民主的崩溃中产生的超级工业社会构成了**彻底无产阶级化的第三个阶段**:我们看到了19世纪的技能知识(savoir-faire)的丧失,20世纪的生活知识(savoir-vivre)的丧失。**在21世纪,我们见证了这个*理论知识*(*savoirs théoriques*, theoretical knowledge)丧失的时代的诞生**——似乎令我们震惊的原因是处在一种*绝对难以想象的发展*中的。

With the ***total automatization*** made possible by digital technology, **theories, those most sublime fruits of idealization and identification, are deemed obsolete**—and along with them, scientific method itself. So at least we are told by Chris Anderson, in *The End of Theory: The Data Deluge Makes the Scientific Method Obsolete*.

随着数字化技术使***总体自动化***(*total automatization*)得以可能,那些作为最卓越的观念化和认同的成果的理论都过时了——同时，科学的方法本身也过时了。这至少是克里斯·安德森（Chris Anderson）① 在《理论的终结：数据洪流淘汰科学方法》（*The End of Theory：The Data Deluge Makes the Scientific Method Obsolete*）一书中告诉我们的。

Founded on the *self-and-auto-production* of digital traces, and *dominated by automatisms* that exploit these traces, hyper-industrial societies are undergoing the proletarianization of theoretical knowledge, just as **broadcasting analogue traces** via television resulted in the **proletarianization of savoir-vivre,** and just as the **submission of the body** of the labourer to **mechanical traces** inscribed in machines resulted in the **proletarianization of savoir-faire.**

建立在数字踪迹的*自主-自动生产*之上的、由使用这些踪迹的*自动主义所主导*的超级工业社会正在经历理论知识的无产阶级化，就像电视的广播模拟踪迹导致生活知识的无产阶级化，就像工人身体向机械踪迹（mechanical traces）的屈服导致技能知识的无产阶级化。

---

① 克里斯·安德森（Chris Anderson, 1961— ）：作家、企业家、美国《连线》杂志（*Wired*）总编辑，曾任职于《自然》《科学》《经济学家》等著名刊物。其代表作有：《长尾理论》（2006）、《免费》（2009）、《创客：新工业革命》（2012）等。——译者注

Just like the written traces in which Socrates already saw the threat of proletarianization that any exteriorisation of knowledge brings with it—the *apparent paradox* being that *the constitution of knowledge depends on the exteriorisation of knowledge* —so too digital, analogue and mechanical traces are what I call tertiary retentions, and I will explain later these terms.

就像苏格拉底在文字踪迹（written traces）中已经看到了无产阶级化的威胁，任何知识的外化（exteriorisation）都将带来这一结果——而*明显矛盾的是知识的建构恰恰依赖于知识的外化*——这样，数字的、模拟的和机械的踪迹就是我所说的第三持存（tertiary retentions）。以后我将解释这些术语。

When Gilles Deleuze referred to what he called " **control societies,** " he was already heralding the arrival of the **hyperindustrial** age. **The destructive capture of attention and desire** is what occurs in and through those control societies that Deleuze described in terms of **the non-coercive modulation exercised by television on consumers** at the end of the twentieth century. These societies of control appear **at the end of the consumerist epoch,** and what they do is to make way for the

transition to the hyper-industrial epoch.

当德勒兹指认他所说的"控制社会（control societies）"时，他就已经预告了超级工业时代的到来。**对注意力和欲望的破坏性捕获**就在德勒兹根据20世纪末**电视对消费者的非强制性调节（the non-coercive modulation）**所描述的控制社会中，并通过这种控制社会发生着。这些控制社会出现在**消费主义时代晚期**，它们要做的就是设法向**超级工业社会时代过渡**。

In the **automated society** of which Deleuze could hardly have been aware, but which he and Félix Guattari anticipated (in particular when they referred to *dividuals*), control undertakes the **mechanical liquidation of discernment**, from the Greek *to krinon*—from *krinein*, a verb that has the same root as *krisis*, decision. **Discernment**, which Kant called **understanding** (*Verstand*), **has been automated and automatized as *analytical* power** that has been **delegated to algorithms**, algorithms that convey formalized instructions through sensors and actuators but **outside of any intuition in the Kantian sense**, that is, **outside of any experience** (this being the situation that occupies Chris Anderson).

德勒兹还没有意识到**自动社会**(**automated society**),但他和瓜塔里预言了它(特别是当他们指认了**分割体**[*dividuals*]的时候)。在自动社会中,控制就是**对洞察力的机械性清算**(**mechanical liquidation of discernment**),从希腊语*判断*(*krinein*)到 *krinon*——*krinein* 这一动词与*决断*(*krisis*,decision)有着相同的词根。**洞察力**,即康德所说的**知性**(**understanding** [*Verstand*])已经被自动化,且被**自动化为依托于算法的分析权力**(***analytical* power**)。算法是通过传感器和执行器来传递形式化指令的,而这都是**在康德意义上的任何直觉、任何经验**(这是克里斯·安德森所讨论的情境)**之外的**。

*

Eight years after the collapse of 2008, it is still not clear how best to characterize this *event*: *crisis*, *mutation*, *metamorphosis*? All these terms are *metaphors*—they still fall short of actual thinking.

2008年崩溃以后的八年里,人们仍然不知道如何最恰当地界定这个*事件*:*危机*,*突变*(*mutation*),*蜕变*(*metamorphosis*)? 所有这些术语都是*隐喻*(*metaphors*)——它们仍然缺乏真正的思考。

Krisis, which has a long history—in Hippocrates it refers to a decisive turning point in the course of an illness—is also **the origin of all critique**, of **all decision** exercised by *to krinon* as **the power to judge on the basis of criteria.**

危机(***Krisis***)有着悠久的历史——在希波克拉底那里,它是指疾病过程中的一个关键性的转折点——它也是**一切批判、一切决断,即根据标准做出判断的权力**(*krinon*)的起源。

Mutation is understood today primarily in relation to **biology**—even if, in French, to be *"mute"* generally refers in everyday life to being transferred to another posting.

突变(***Mutation***)在今天主要是从**生物学**的意义上来理解的——即使在法语中,"*切除*(*mute*)"在日常生活的意义上也是指被从一个位置转移到另一个位置。

Metamorphosis is a **zoological term** that comes from the Greek—by way of Ovid.

蜕变(*Metamorphosis*)是一个**动物学术语**,它来自希腊语,由奥维德(Ovid)① 引介而来。

Seven years after this event, it seems that **the *proletarianization of minds*, and more precisely, the *proletarianization of the noetic faculties of theorization and in this sense of scientific, moral, aesthetic and political deliberation*—combined with the proletarianization of** sensibility **and affect in the twentieth century, and with the proletarianization of the gestures of the worker in the nineteenth century—is both the *trigger for* and the *result of* this continuing "crisis."** As a result, **no decisions are taken**, nor do we arrive at any turning point, any "**bifurcation**" for speaking with Deleuze's words, that is **a negentropic event** as we will see later. Whereas, **all of the toxic aspects that lie at the origins of this crisis continue to be consolidated.**

2008年崩溃后的七年里,似乎*心灵的无产阶级化*(*proletarianization of minds*),更准确地说,*理论化的智力能力的无产阶级阶级化*(*the proletarianization of the noetic faculties of theorization*),在科学的、伦理的、审美

---

① 奥维德(Publius Ovidius Naso,公元前43年—公元前17年/18年未能确认):古罗马诗人,与贺拉斯、卡图卢斯和维吉尔齐名。代表作:《变形记》《爱的艺术》《爱情三论》等。——译者注

的和政治的协商意义上——它与 20 世纪的感性和情感的无产阶级化，与 19 世纪的工人姿态的无产阶级化是一致的——既是这种持续的"危机"的*诱因*（trigger），又是它的*结果*。结果，我们没有做任何决断，也没有抵达任何转折点或德勒兹所说的"分叉点（bifurcation）"，即我们后面将会看到的一种负熵事件（a negentropic event）。然而，蕴含在这场危机源头中的一切有害方面都继续被强化了。

When a triggering factor is also an outcome, **we find ourselves in a spiral.** This spiral can be very fruitful and worthwhile, or **it can enclose us**—*absent new criteria*—**in a vicious circle** that we describe as a "downward **spiral**", a "spirale du pire", that takes us **from bad to worse.**

当原因亦即结果的时候，我们发现自己处在一种螺旋（spiral）之中。这种螺旋可能是卓有成效而值得的，也可能把我们封闭在——缺乏新的标准——恶性循环之中，我们将其描述为一种"向下**螺旋**（downward **spiral**）"，一种"更坏的螺旋（spirale du pire）"，它将我们推向更糟糕的境地。

The *post-larval state* in which we have left the crisis of

2008 means we should refer to it in terms of metamorphosis (rather than mutation, **what is going on here is not biological**, even if biology comes into play via biotechnology, and, in certain respects, in a quasi-proletarianized way). **This does not mean that there is no *krisis*** , or that we need not take account of the **critical labour** for which it calls. It means that **THIS CRITICAL LABOUR IS PRECISELY WHAT THIS METAMORPHOSIS SEEMS TO RENDER IMPOSSIBLE, thanks precisely to the fact that it** consists *above all* **in the proletarianization of theoretical knowledge**, which is critical knowledge. It is for this reason that I propose **understanding the enduring nature of this crisis on the basis of the metaphor of the chrysalis.**

我们已将 2008 年危机停留在*后幼虫状态*（*post-larval state*），这意味着我们应该将其看作一种蜕变（而不是突变：**这里所说的不是生物学上的突变**，即使生物学是通过生物技术［biotechnology］、在某些方面是以准-无产阶级化［quasi-proletarianized］的方式得以进行的）。**这并不意味着没有危机**，或者我们不需要考虑它所呼吁的**批判性劳动**（critical labour）。也就是说，**这种批判性劳动（CRITICAL**

LABOUR）恰恰是这种蜕变似乎不可能提供的东西①，也正是由于这样的事实，因此蜕变首先在于理论知识即批判性知识（critical knowledge）**的无产阶级化**。正是出于这个原因，我认为要基于这种关于蛹（chrysalis）的比喻来理解这次危机的持久本质。

The ***stupefying situation*** in which the current experience of **automatic society** consists establishes **a new mental context (stupefaction) within which systemic stupidity undoubtedly proliferates (as *functional stupidity*, drive-based capitalism, and industrial populism), but which can also be viewed in relation to a NEW CONCERN** —which, *if it is not turned into panic*, and instead becomes **a fertile *skepsis*, could turn out to be the *beginning of a new understanding of the situation*** —and **the genesis of new criteria, or categories**: this is the question of what I call ***categorial invention***. And it is also the question of new apprehension of the questions of bifurcation, that is of negentropic events into the Anthropocene apprehend as an entropocene.

当下自动社会实践的*混沌状态*（*stupefying situation*）

---

① 此段文字在原文为全部字母大写，在中文中没有表现这一字体标识。——译者注

建构了一种新的精神语境（即麻木呆滞［stupefaction］），在这种语境下，系统性愚昧无疑是激增了（功能性愚昧、以驱力为基础的资本主义［drive-based capitalism］和工业平民主义［industrial populism］），但这也可以从一种新角度（NEW CONCERN）——如果它没有转变为恐慌（*panic*），而是变为一种丰富的*怀疑*(fertile *skepsis*)，就有可能产生对这种状况的新的理解的开始——和新标准或范畴的开端来看待这一现象：这就是我所说的*范畴发明*（*categorial invention*）问题。而且，这也是对分叉点（bifurcation）问题的新的理解问题，即把人类纪中的负熵活动（negentropic events）理解为一种熵纪（entropocene）的问题。

ENTROPOCENE

This **new understanding or intelligence** would be **that which**, inverting the toxic logic of the *pharmakon*, would give rise to a *new hyper-industrial age constituting an automatic society founded on de-proletarianization*, that is, **on negentropy**—and **which would provide an exit from the chrysalis of** *noetic hymenoptera*①—based on the valorisation of positive externalities and capacities (in Amartya Sen's sense), that is, on a contributive economy of pollination.

这种新的理解或智慧将会颠倒**药**的**毒性逻辑**（the toxic logic of the *pharmakon*），从而产生一个**新的超级工业时代**（*new hyper-industrial age*），这个时代建构了**一个基于去无产阶级化**(*de-proletarianization*)**，即负熵之上的自动社会**——它将提供一条从**智性昆虫**②的蛹（the chrysalis of *noetic hymenoptera*）中蜕变出来的出路——而这一路径是**基于**（阿玛蒂亚·桑［Amartya Sen］意义上的）**积极的外部性和能力的增殖，即基于一种捐赠性的传粉经济**（a contributive economy of pollination）之上。

---

① French Wikipedia entry on hymenoptera: "The order hymenoptera includes herbivores, pollinators, and a wide range of entomophagous insects that play a central role in maintaining natural equilibrium. The entomophagous insects comprise the majority of parasitoids (43% of hymenoptera species that have been described) but also predators. The actual number of hymenoptera is estimated at somewhere between one and three million species, divided into a hundred families. Many species have not yet been described, or even discovered."

② 法文维基百科对膜翅目昆虫的词条解释是："膜翅目昆虫包括食草动物、传粉昆虫以及种类繁多的食虫性昆虫，后者在维系自然平衡中起到主要作用。食虫性昆虫占了拟寄生昆虫的大多数（占膜翅目昆虫的43%），也是食肉动物。据估算，膜翅目昆虫大约有100万到300万种，分为100个科。很多种类的膜翅目昆虫还尚未被研究或发现。"

The **proletarianization of the gestures of work** amounts to the **proletarianization of the conditions of the worker's** *sub*-sistence.

Sub-sistence

The **proletarianization of sensibility**, of sensory life, and the proletarianization **of social relations**, all of which being replaced by conditioning, amounts to the **proletarianization of the conditions of the citizen's** *ex*-sistence.

Sub-sistence
Ex-sistence

The **proletarianization of minds or spirits**, that is, of the noetic faculties enabling theorization and deliberation, is the **proletarianization of the conditions of scientific** *con*-sistence (including the human and social sciences).

Sub-sistence
Ex-sistence
Con-sistence

工作姿势的无产阶级化（proletarianization of the

gestures of work）发展为工人的*屈-在*（*sub*-sistence）状况的无产阶级化。

一切都受条件限制的**感情**（sensibility）、**感性生活**（sensory life）**和社会关系的无产阶级化**发展为**市民的*外-在*（*ex*-sistence）状况的无产阶级化**。

心灵或精神的无产阶级化，即能够进行理论化和慎思的智力能力的无产阶级化，是**科学*共-存*（*con*-sistence，包括各种人文社会科学）条件的无产阶级化**。

In the hyper-industrial stage, *hyper-control* is established through a process of generalized automatization. It thus represents a step beyond the control-through-modulation discovered and analyzed by Deleuze. Now, the **noetic faculties of theorization and deliberation are short-circuited by the *current operator of proletarianization*, which is *digital tertiary retention*, or mnemotechnical artefact**—just as **analogue tertiary retention** was in the twentieth century the operator of the proletarianization of savoir-vivre, and just as **mechanical tertiary retention** was in the nineteenth century the operator of the proletarianization of savoir-faire.

在超级工业时代，*超级控制*（*hyper-control*）是通过普遍的自动化过程建立的。因此，它代表着超越德勒兹所发现和分析的调节-控制（control-through-modulation）的一步。现在，这种理论化和慎思的智力能力因*当前的无产阶级化主导因素*（*current operator of proletarianization*）而短路了，这种无产阶级化即*数字第三持存*（*digital tertiary retention*），或记忆技术制品（mnemotechnical artefact）——正如**模拟第三持存**（analogue tertiary retention）是导致 20 世纪生活知识（savoir-vivre）的无产阶级化的主导因素，**机械第三持存**（mechanical tertiary retention）是导致 19 世纪技能知识（savoir-faire）的无产阶级化的主导因素。

By *artificially retaining something through the material and spatial copying of a mnesic and temporal element*, tertiary retention modifies the relations between the psychic retentions of *perception* that Husserl referred to as *primary* retentions, and the psychic retentions of *memory* that he called *secondary* retentions.

通过对一种记忆要素和时间要素进行物质的、空间的复制而人为地保存某物，第三持存就改变了胡塞尔所指认的作为*原生*持存的心理*知觉*持存和作为第二持存的心理*记忆*持存之间的关系。

What is called "reason", and more generally, what is

called thinking is a form of attention, and that attention is itself an arrangement operating between what Husserl referred to as retentions (R, memories) and protentions (P, expectations), via the intermediary of **technical** retentions, that is, mnemotechnics, which I call **tertiary retentions** (this is not Husserl's views of course, except in his *Origin of geometry*): **alphabetical writing**, like **digital writing**, is a type of tertiary retention. **Attentional forms**, which constitute ways of thinking, are **arrangements of retentions and protentions** made **possible** by **mnemotechnical forms of memorization.**

$$A=R3\ (R/P)$$

所谓的"理性",更一般地说,所谓的思考就是一种注意形式(form of attention)。注意本身是一种在胡塞尔所说的持存(retentions)(R,记忆)和前摄(protentions)(P,期望)之间运行的安排,这种安排需要借助**技术**持存(**technical** retentions)即记忆存储器(mnemotechnics)的中介,我称之为**第三持存**(**tertiary retentions**,当然,除了他的《几何学起源》[*Origin of geometry*]之外,胡塞尔没有表达这样的观点):**字母文字**(**alphabetical writing**),比如**数字化文字**,就是一种第三持存。构造思路的**注意形式**(**attentional forms**)是持存和前摄之间的各种安排,而这又是借助记忆存储器式的记忆形式(**mnemotechnical** forms of memorization）而成为可能的。

Thinking, **in all its forms**, is a temporal fabric of what Husserl called *primary and secondary* **retentions and protentions**. A temporal flux or flow, such as **a speech that you might listen to**, as in fact you are doing at this very moment, can only constitute itself as such because it is **an aggregation of what Husserl called primary retentions**. In the course of this speech that I am delivering before you, and that you seem to be listening to, you **retain** in a **"primary"** way each of the elements that are presented. "Primary" here means that **each element that presents itself in each instant aggregates itself to the element that follows it in the next instant**, and is **retained** in it, with which it forms **the "now" of the temporal flow**—hence **phonemes** that aggregate to form a **word**, **words** that aggregate to form a **sentence**, **sentences** that aggregate to form a **paragraph**, and so on—so that a **unity of meaning** is formed. These aggregations that accumulate one upon the other form what Husserl called primary retentions.

一切形式的*思考*都是一种胡塞尔所说的*原生持存、第二持存和前摄*（*primary and secondary* retentions and protentions）的时间结构。一种时间之流，比如你在听一场演讲，而实际上，你在这个瞬间所听到的东西，只能以这种方式建构它自身，因为它是**一种胡塞尔所说的许多原生持存的聚合**。现在，我正在给你们上课，你好像在听，你以"**原生〔持存〕**"的方式**保存**下每一个被发出的要素。"原生"在这里意味着**每一个在每一瞬间中展现自身的要素都将会汇聚到紧随其后的下一瞬间的要素中，并被保留**在这一要素中。由此，它就形成**时间之流中的"现在"**——因此，**许多音素（phonemes）聚合成一个词，许多词聚合成一个句子，许多句子聚合成一个段落**，如此等等——这样，**一个意义统一体（unity of meaning）**就形成了。这些一个接一个积累起来的集合就形成了胡塞尔所说的原生持存。

These primary retentions are, however, **selections**—they are *retained* only on **the basis of retentional** *criteria*, criteria that are **formed in the course of my prior experience**. And my experience is, precisely, **an accumulation of** *secondary retentions*, which are former primary retentions that subsequently become past, and which constitute the stuff of my memory.

然而，这些原生持存就是**诸多选择（selections）**：它们只是**根据持存的*标准*（retentional *criteria*）**而被*保留*下来，而这些标准是**在我之前的经验过程中形成的**。准确地说，我的经验是**一种*第二持存*的积累（an accumulation of** *secondary retentions*），而第二持存又是先前的、转瞬即逝的原生持存，并构成我的记忆的材料。

**THIRD COURSE
28 MARCH 2016
/**

Reading Marx and Heidegger
in the Anthropocene
Retentions, Protentions and Knowledge

**第 三 讲
2016.3.28**
在人类纪阅读马克思和海德格尔：
持存、前摄和知识

Each and every one of you, who are currently **listening to me**, will be hearing in what I say **something different**, and this is so because **what I say is a flow of primary retentions from out of which each of you make a different selection**, to the degree that each of you have **different memories composed of different secondary retentions**, resulting in **different criteria for retaining and understanding** what I tell you.

当下你们**正在听我讲课**的每一个人所听到的东西是**不一样的**,这是因为**我所说的是一种原生持存之流**(a flow of primary retentions),从中你们每个人做了不同选择,因而在某种程度上,你们每个人有着**由不同的第二持存所构成的不同记忆**,结果就形成了**不同的标准来保留和理解**我对你们说的东西。

We can summarize and formalize those by saying that, if the relationship between R and P and R1 and R2 is conditioned by what I called last week R3, then we should say that, each one of you pays *attention* to what I say, therefore, in a singular way. But **what nonetheless *unites* your different ways of hearing what I say, and thus ensures the possibility of forming an *agreement* between all your various understandings of what I tell you, is a *rational attentional form*.**

我们可以将这些现象概括和形式化为这样一种表述：如果 R（Retention，持存）和 P（Protention，前摄）之间的关系以及 R1（原生持存）和 R2（第二持存）之间的关系受到上周我所说 R3 的制约，那么我们可以说，你们每个人都以独特的方式*注意*我所说的东西。但尽管如此，**那种将你们听我说话的不同方式*统一*起来，从而保证在你们对我说的东西的不同理解之间有可能形成一种*同意*（*agreement*）的东西，就是一种*理性注意形式*（*rational attentional form*）。**

The latter is formed through **apodictic experience** (of which geometry is the canonical example)—on the basis of which my speech tries to bring about an agreement between you. According to Husserl, in *Origin of Geometry*, this is made possible by the alphabetic writing, that is what I call myself the literal tertiary retention in *Technics and Time, 2*.

后者是通过**必然经验**(**apodictic experience**)(几何学就是一个典型例子)而构成的——正是基于这种必然经验,我的演说才试图在你们之间达成一种同意。根据胡塞尔的《几何学的起源》一书,它是以字母文字(alphabetic writing)的方式而成为可能的,这就是我在《技术与时间·2》中所说的"文字第三持存(literal tertiary retention)"。

The literal tertiary retention has a specific property that is its capacity to synthetize orthothetically,

orthothetically

this meaning exactly, an oral linguistic statement—for example, this oral linguistic statement that I now produce myself.

**for example, this oral
linguistic statement
that I now produce
myself**

文字第三持存有一种特殊的性质,即它能够以确正的方式(orthothetically)进行合成。确切地说,这是一种口头语言表达（oral linguistic statement），比如我现在自己发出的口头语言表达。

"Orthothetic" comes from two Greek words, "orthos"

$$Ορθος$$

and "thesis".

$$θέσις$$

In his text dedicated to Plato's understanding of truth, as it appears in *The Republic*, Heidegger claims that Plato forgot the meaning of "aletheia"

$$ἀλήθεια$$

by interpreting it as "orthotès"

$$Ὀρθοθης$$

that is exactitude. I personally believe that
    • this was made possible by the specific orthothetical character of the literal tertiary retention;
    • this produced also the contrary, because of what I described as what I called the "differential identity".

differential identity

Orthothetic 来自两个希腊文：orthos（Oρθos，确正）和 thesis（θέσis，命题）。在海德格尔讨论柏拉图对真理的理解的文本中，比如《理想国》中的真理观念，海德格尔认为，当柏拉图将真理解释为 orthotès（Ὀρθοθης）时，他就忘记了真理（aletheia, truth, αλήθεια）的意义，这是对的。我个人认为，

- 文字第三持存的特殊的确正特点使它成为可能的；
- 而这也产生了相反的东西，这是因为我所说的"差异的同一性（differential identity）"。

The differential identity is what happens when, for example, re-reading a book, or an article, or notes I took the week before, I interpret it **differently from the first time.**

这种差异的同一性会在这种情况下发生，比如，重读一本书或一篇文章，或者我一周前写下的笔记，我对它的**解释与第一次是不同的。**

I believe that the specificity of the **cumulative knowledge that apodictic geometry is,** and where the word apodictic, coming from the Greek word "apodeixis" ἀπόδειξις

means **based on a strictly formalized condition of demonstration**, gives its meaning at the Greek experience of *aletheia* in general, I believe that **this, then, comes from the experience of the literal tertiary retention** as it constitutes both

- an "orthothesis"

orthothesis

that is an **exact transmission of the logic reasoning of a thinker word by word,** that is also step by step, letter by letter, **logic** meaning here first of all **linguistic,** that is, **made by the stuff of words,** and **the experience of the literal tertiary retention** as it constitutes also and in the same time

- a "differential identity"

differential identity

that is, **a recording the repetition of which always produces a difference.** How the repetition of the same reading is it capable to produce a difference, this is also the stake of the book *Difference and Repetition*.

This production of differences being a process of interpretation that, in Greece, is called

'Ερμηνεία

a word coming from the name of a God, Hermès.

我认为，**积累性知识（cumulative knowledge）（必然的几何学〔apodictic geometry〕就是这种知识）的特殊性**，以及这里提到的来自希腊文"apodeixis（证明、证据）"的 apodictic 这个词，都意味着它是**基于证明的严格的形式化条件**，从而获得了希腊语意义上的*一般真理*（aletheia in general）的经验。我认为，这种特性是**源自于文字第三持存的经验**，因为它既构成一种确正命题（orthothesis），也构成一种差异的同一性（differential identity）。前者（确正命题）是**一个思想家一字一字地、一步一步地乃至一个字母一个字母地进行准确的逻辑推理**。这里，"**逻辑的**"首先意味着"**语言的**（linguistic）"，即由**词汇材料和文字第三持存的经验**所构成的东西。后者（差异的同一性）是指**一种总是生产差异的重复性记录**。反复读同一读物如何能够产生一种差异，这也是德勒兹《差异与重复》这本书的任务。

差异的产生就是一个解读的过程，用希腊文来说就是 'Ερμηνεία，这个词来自一个神的名字，Hermès。

What kind of tertiary retention a Chinese character is, and what type of differentiation in repetition does it make possible? It is a mystery for me because I am not capable to read and write Chinese characters. Now, I am convinced that **the question of** Chinese **origin of algebraic mathematics comes from this type of ideographic tertiary retention**, as is what said by Freret, a French sinologist of the nineteenth century.

Chinese characters are immediate signs of the ideas which they express. One would think that the system of writing was invented by mutes, ignorant of the use of speech. We may compare the characters of which it is composed to the algebraic signs which express relations in our mathematical books. Let a geometrical demonstration, expressed in algebraic characters, be presented to ten mathematicians of different countries, they will all understand it alike, and yet they will not understand the words by which those ideas are expressed in speech. The same thing takes place in China; the writing is not only common to all the inhabitants of that great country, who speak dialects different from each other, but also to the Japanese, the Tonquinese, and the Cochinchinese, whose languages are entirely distinct from the Chinese.

汉字是一种什么样的第三持存呢？汉字在重复中可能会产生何种差异呢？这对我来说还是个谜，因为我不会读，也不会写汉字。现在，我确信中国的**代数学（algebraic mathematics）**起源问题是来自一种表意性的第三持存（ideographic tertiary retention），正如一位19世纪的法国汉学家弗雷烈（Freret）所说的那样：

> 汉字是他们表达思想所用的直接符号。有人可能会认为这套文字体系是由一群不懂语音的沉默的人发明的。我们可以将这些最基本的汉字比作我们数学书中那些用来表示关系的代数符号。将一个用代数符号表达的几何证明（geometrical demonstration）展示给十个来自不同国家的数学家，他们都能够理解得差不多，但他们并不理解用说话方式来表达这些思想时所用的语词。同样的事情就发生在中国，这种文字（汉字）不仅对于那个伟大国度里彼此说着不同方言的所有居民来说是共通的，而且对于拥有与汉语完全不同的

语言的日本人、东京人①和南圻人来说也是共通的。

So, we could say that **Greek alphabetic letters**, that are **literal tertiary retentions**, made possible the **apodictic development of Greek geometry**, whereas **Chinese ideographic characters** made possible **the algebraic development of mathematics**.

所以,我们可以说,**希腊字母文字**(Greek alphabetic letters)是一种**文字第三持存**(literal tertiary retentions),它使得**希腊的几何学获得显著发展**成为可能。而**中国的表意文字**(ideographic characters)使**代数学的发展**成为可能。

Here I must point out that there is in the west a debate concerning Chinese geometry, that begins with Mo Jing.

This debate turns around the status that we can and must give to this geometrical object coming from Chinese geometry, and if the figural explanation of the geometrical reasoning, as we can see it here can be considered as a demonstration, and more precisely, as an apodictic demonstration.

---

① "Tonquin"是西方人对越南首都河内之旧称"东京"的英译称呼。在历史上,河内历经多次更名,其中1428年越南后黎朝建立,将其称为"东京",1831年越南阮朝的明命帝又将其改称为"河内",并一直沿用到今天。因此,此处的"东京人"是指越南河内地区的人。——译者注

This is for example the stake of this text, talking about diagrammatic demonstration, and citing Joseph Needham, who claimed that there was no demonstration properly speaking in Chinese geometry.

The "Piling-Up of Rectangles": The Pythagorean Theorem in China.

The Pythagorean theorem is generally held to be one of the most important results in the early history of mathematics, from it came important discoveries in theoretical geometry as well as practical mensuration. We saw in chapter 4 how the Mesopotamians' understanding of geometry, based on similar triangles and circles, was enhanced by the discovery of the Pythagorean result, and how their algorithmic procedure for extracting square roots of "irregular" (irrational) numbers was also based on this result. In China too, a study of the properties of the right-angled triangle had a considerable impact on mathematics.

The earliest extant Chinese text on astronomy and mathematics, the *Zhou Bi*, is notable for a diagrammatic demonstration of the Pythagorean (or *gou gu*) theorem. Needham's translation of the relevant passage is illustrated by figure 7.1a, drawn from the original text, who claimed that there was no demonstration properly speaking in Chinese geometry.①

这里，我必须指出，西方关于中国几何学的争论始于《墨经》。这场争论发生了好的转向，即认为我们必须给予中国几何学的几何学对象应有的地位。如果可以对几何推理进行图形解释的话，就像我们这里可以看到的那样，那么，这种推理就可以被认作一种证明，更准确地说，一种必然性证明。比如，这是乔治·G. 约瑟夫（George Gheverghese Joseph）援引李约瑟（Joseph Needham）来讨论图解证明的一段关键文字：

"矩形的堆积"：中国的毕达哥拉斯定理（Pythagorean Theorem）。

毕达哥拉斯定理通常被看作早期数学史上最重要的成果之一，基于这一定理在理论几何学和应用测量学中产生了许多重要的发现。我们在第

---

① 参见 George Gheverghese Joseph, *The Crest of the Peacock: Non-European Roots of Mathematics*. Princeton: Princeton University Press, 2011, p. 248.——译者注

四章中就能看到美索不达米亚人基于相似三角形和圆而对几何学的理解是如何由于毕达哥拉斯定理的发现而获得发展的，以及他们关于"不规则"（无理）数的开平方的演算步骤是如何建立在这一发现之上的。同样地，在中国，关于直角三角形性质的研究对数学产生了相当重要的影响。

现存最早的研究天文学和数学的中文文献《周髀》对毕达哥拉斯（或勾股）定理所做的一种图解证明是值得注意的。李约瑟对其中相关段落的翻译可以通过从原始文本中摘取的图表 7.1a 加以说明。

不过，他认为中国的几何学没有严格意义上的证明。

Anyway, let us continue our analysis of what tertiary retention is, and why this stuff is so important for our goals in this seminar.

不管怎样，让我们来继续分析什么是第三持存，为什么它对于我们研讨课的讨论目标如此重要。

The *literal*（that is, lettered）*tertiary retention* , that emerged around eight hundred B. C. in the Mediterranean Basin, made possible **an attentional form through which a**

rational and logical—in the meaning of the Greeks—<u>transindividuation process</u> is produced.

大约出现于公元前 8 世纪的地中海流域的*文字（即字母的）*第三持存，使得这样一种注意形式成为可能，即通过这种注意形式，产生出一种*理性的*和*逻辑的*——在希腊语意义上的——<u>*超个体化过程*（*transindividuation process*）</u>。

To clarify this point, I must introduce concepts that derive from **Gilbert Simondon**, who showed in this book that **to individuate** *psychically is always to contribute to a collective individuation*, and that **this psycho-social individuation generates the** *transindividual*, that is, shared *meanings*, which are, equally, <u>**collective**</u> **secondary retentions**, and **which always themselves presuppose** *supports*, **or carriers, that enable them to be transmitted through time.** These supports or carriers are **technical objects in general**, and **hypomnesic technics in particular**, that are **hypomnesic tertiary retentions.**

**hypomnesic
tertiary
retentions**

为了阐明这一点，我必须引入来自吉尔伯特·西蒙栋

《形式与信息概念中的个体化》（*L'individuation à la lumière des notions de forme et d'information*）一书的一些概念。他说，**心理上的个体化总会促成一种集体的个体化**（*collective individuation*），而这种心理-社会的个体化就会**产生超个体之物**（**the** *transindividual*），即共享的意义（shared meanings），相当于<u>集体的</u>**第二持存**（<u>collective</u> **secondary retentions**），它们总是自我预设**支撑**（*supports*）或载体（carriers），从而使它们能够穿越时间传递下去。这些支撑或载体就是**一般的技术客体**（technical objects in general）和**特殊的超级记忆技术**（hypomnesic technics in particular），即**超级第三持存**（hypomnesic tertiary retentions）。

Hypomnesic technologies, that are technologies **making possible the transmission of mental contents**, this beginning with the rupestrial drawings in the caves of the Upper Paleolithic, hypomnesic technologies such as writing, ideographic or alphabetic, amount to *spatial projections* of events that are firstly psychic, and *as such temporal*.

超级记忆技术就是那种**使精神内容的传递成为可能的技术**，这些技术发端于旧石器时代晚期的洞穴壁画。超级记忆技术，比如表意文字或字母文字，就是**各种活动的空间投射**（*spatial projections*），这些活动首先是心理的

(**psychic**),*同样是时间的*(*temporal*)。

More generally, **all technical supports, objects and practices are the results of a process of *technical individuation*.** This is why **psychic and collective individuation is always** *also* **a technical individuation.**

Technical individuation is concretized as technical system in the meaning given to this expression by Bertrand Gille's *Histoire des Techniques* and which is the concretisation of exosomatisation.

更一般地说,一切技术支撑、客体和实践都是*技术个体化过程*(**process of** *technical individuation*)的结果。这就是为什么心理个体化和集体个体化*也*总是一种技术个体化。

从贝特兰·吉尔(Bertrand Gille)在《技术史》(*Histoire des Techniques*)一书中所赋予这一表达的意义来看,技术个体化就被具体化为一种技术体系,即外在化的具体化(the concretisation of exosomatisation)。

This means that **noetic psychic individuation, that is, thinking, is** *conditioned* **by technical individuation**—but not determined by it: the technical artefact always opens a field of **indefinite possibilities.** This field of possibilities ranges from the worst to the best because **the technical artefact**—for example, writing—**is a *pharmakon*,**

$$\varphi άρμακον$$

a poison that can become a remedy, or vice versa.

这意味着智性心理的个体化（noetic psychic individuation）即思考是以技术个体化为*条件*的——但前者并不是由后者决定的：技术人造物（technical artefact）总能打开一片充满**无限可能性**（indefinite possibilities）的领域。这片可能性领域包括从最坏到最好的各种可能性，因为**技术人造物——比如文字——是一种药**（pharmakon, *φάρμακον*）：一种可治病的毒药，反之亦然。

Over time, **tertiary retention evolves**, for example, rupestrial or low relief tertiary retentions become written tertiary retention, and this leads to **modifications of the *play* between primary retentions and secondary retentions**, resulting in *processes of transindividuation* that are each time specific, that is, **specific epochs of what Simondon called the *transindividual*.**

随着时间的流逝，**第三持存**不断发展，比如从石洞壁画或半浮雕第三持存发展为文字第三持存，这导致**原生持**

存和第二持存之间的*作用*发生变化，这就形成了在每一时代中的具体的*超个体化过程*（*processes of transindividuation*），即西蒙栋所说的具体时代的*超个体之物*（the *transindividual*）。

In such an evolution analog technologies of, or phonography, and then, cinematography, television are analog orthothetic recordings, whereas computers and digital networks are digital orthothetic tertiary retentions.

模拟技术经历了这样一个演变过程，即表音速记、电影摄制和电视都是模拟确正性记录（analog orthothetic recordings），而电脑和数字化网络则是数字确正性第三持存（digital orthothetic tertiary retentions）。

In the course of processes of transindividuation, founded on successive epochs of tertiary retention, **shared meanings are formed by psychic individuals who thereby constitute collective individuals, and what we call "societies". The meanings formed during transindividuation processes, and shared by psychic individuals within collective individuals of all kinds, constitute the transindividual as the set of COLLECTIVE SECONDARY RETENTIONS through which collective PROTENTIONS** are formed—the *expectations* that typify that epoch.

在超个体化过程中，基于连续时代的第三持存，共享的意义（shared meanings）是通过心理的个人形成的。由此，这些心理的个人构成集体的个人，即我们所说的"社会"。这些意义在超个体化过程中形成，并被在各种集体个人中的心理的个人所共享，于是这种超个体之物（the transindividual）就被建构成为<u>集体第二持存（COLLECTIVE SECONDARY RETENTIONS）</u>的集合。凭借这种集体第二持存，<u>集体前摄（collective PROTENTIONS）</u>就形成了——这种集体前摄就是代表那个时代典型特征的*期望*（*expectations*）。

If, according to the Chris Anderson article previously referred to, so-called "big data" heralds the "end of theory"—big data technology designating what is also called "high-performance computing" carried out on massive amounts of data, **whereby the treatment of data in the form of digital tertiary retentions occurs *in real time* (at the speed of light) and on a *global scale* and at the level of billions of gigabytes of data**, operating through **data-capture systems that are located everywhere around the planet and in almost every relational system that constitutes a society** — it is because **DIGITAL**

TERTIARY RETENTION AND THE ALGORITHMS THAT ALLOW IT TO BE BOTH PRODUCED AND EXPLOITED THEREBY ALSO MAKE IT POSSIBLE FOR *REASON AS A SYNTHETIC FACULTY TO BE SHORT-CIRCUITED* thanks to the EXTREMELY HIGH SPEEDS at which this automated ANALYTICAL FACULTY OF *UNDERSTANDING* is capable of operating.

如果根据前面提到的克里斯·安德森（Chris Anderson）的文章，所谓的"大数据"预示着"理论的终结"——大数据技术也就是对大量数据的"高性能计算（high-performance computing）"，由此以数字第三持存（digital tertiary retentions）的形式进行的数据处理能够（以光速）*实时地*（*in real time*）、在全球范围内、以处理几十亿千兆数据的水平进行着，并通过遍布全球每一个角落、渗入社会几乎每个体系的数据收集系统运行着——这是因为数字第三持存和算法使"大数据"能够得以产生和开发（BOTH PRODUCED AND EXPLOITED）出来。然而，理性作为一种综合能力（*A SYNTHETIC FACULTY*）也有可能因为"大数据"具有极速运转的自动的*知性*分析能力而发生*短路*。

Because as we already have seen, in *The Critique of Pure*

Reason, Kant explains how and why understanding, that is *Verstand*, and reason, that is *Vernunft*, are two different and irreducible dimensions of knowledge, understanding being analytic, and reason synthetic.

因为正如我们已经看到的,在《纯粹理性批判》中,康德解释了*知性*(*Verstand*)和*理性*(*Vernunft*)如何和为什么是知识的两个不同的而又不可再分的维度,知性在于分析,而理性在于综合。

*

Now, let us have a look on these questions if we go back to Engels and Marx first and foremost claim, that is, according to me, the exosomatic situation of human beings.

现在,如果我们回到恩格斯和马克思首次提出的人类的外在化情境问题,我们就可以探讨一下这些问题。

*

Hegel saw and showed that the development of mind

and spirit, of that is in German called *Geist*, is a process of exteriorisation or externalisation of mind, or spirit, into what he called the objective spirit, based on objective memory that I call myself tertiary retention. But for Hegel, this "moment" of externalisation was only a moment, that could be overcome by dialectic as the moment of *Aufhebung*, in German, that was understood by Hegel as the moment of re-internalization of the exteriority dissolving this exteroirity into what Hegel called the absolute spirit. All of this was for Hegel the result of what he presented as a **speculative dialectic based on what he called the speculative proposition.**

黑格尔看到，思想和精神（*Geist*）的发展是思想或精神的外化或客观化的过程，这个精神就是他所说的基于客观记忆的客观精神——我称之为第三持存。但是对黑格尔来说，外化"环节"只是一个可以被辩证法作为*扬弃*（*Aufhebung*）的环节而克服的环节，在德语语境中，黑格尔将其理解为消除外在性、将外在性重新内化进绝对精神的环节。对黑格尔来说，所有这一切都是**基于他所说的思辨命题（speculative proposition）之上的思辨辩证法**的结果。

For Engels and Marx, as they tell us in *The German*

Ideology, Hegel's philosophy belongs to what they call german idealism; this one inherited the ideological concepts of Platonic and more generally Greek idealism, based on the theory of ideas proposed by Plato in *The Republic*.

对于马克思和恩格斯来说,正如他们在《德意志意识形态》中告诉我们的,黑格尔哲学属于德国唯心主义,它承袭了柏拉图和更广泛意义上的希腊唯心主义的意识形态观念,并以柏拉图在《理想国》中提出的观念论为基础。

The *materialist* **version** of the **Hegelian speculative dialectic** understands **exteriorisation as** *materialization*, and the latter **as the** *technical self-production* **of humanity by its "means" of production**, while for the first time **posing in an explicit way the question of** *proletarianization*, **that is**, the question **of the** *destruction of knowledge that results from its exteriorisation*, the latter being nevertheless **the fundamental condition of the constitution of all knowledge.**

他们对**黑格尔思辨辩证法**所做的*唯物主义改造*(*materialist version*)就是**将外化**(exteriorisation)**理解为***物化*(*materialization*),后者就是利用生产"资料"进行人类的*技术自我生产*(*technical self-production*),同时第一次明确提出了无产阶级化问题,即*由知识的外化所导致的知识破坏*问题。然而,知识的外化又是*一切知识得以建立的基本条件*。

In the *Communist Manifesto* indeed, proletarianization of the manual workers is described as a loss of their knowledge, that has passed into the means of production that machines are. And Engels and Marx say that this process of proletarianization will progressively reach all the layers of the population.

在《共产党宣言》中,手工工人的无产阶级化被描述为他们的知识的丧失,因为他们的知识已经转入生产资料(机器)中。马克思和恩格斯认为,无产阶级化的过程将会逐步扩展到所有阶层。

Showing that the externalisation of knowing is a proletarianization, as it is a loss of knowledge, **dialectic materialism rediscovered the initial question of the *pharmakon***, where Socrates shows that writing as an externalisation of memory can be also a loss of memory, even if the externalisation is the condition of constitution of knowledge and of the memory in which it consists as the transmission across generations of their experience as accumulated knowledge. As you maybe anticipate, we will refind these questions when reading the *Grundrisse*.

通过表明知识的外化就是一种无产阶级化，因为它也是一种知识的丧失，**辩证唯物主义再次揭示了*药*的原初问题**，即苏格拉底所指出的文字作为一种记忆的外化同时也是记忆的丧失，虽然这种外化是知识和记忆建构的条件，其中，人们的经验作为积累的知识代代相传。正如你们所期待的，我们将在阅读《大纲》时重新回到这个问题。

So, in this interpretation, **the question of proletarianization would be a new version of Socrates' question of the *pharmakon*. And yet,** *this materialism produced no pharmacology.* It continued to understand technics as a means, through which "toxic" processes (such as proletarianization, or its consequence, pauperization) are only the translations of class struggle as relations of production, that can be overcome, this meaning that the toxicity of the pharmakon can be eliminated. On the contrary, I believe that this one can never be eliminated. But it can be fought—and this combat is the one of knowledge. But it is too early for seeing this question, towards which we will come back later.

**所以，在这种解读中，无产阶级化问题将成为苏格拉底的*药*的问题的新版本。然而，*这种唯物主义没有产生药理学*（*pharmacology*）：它仍然将技术（technics）理解为手段（means），借助这种手段，"毒性"过程（比如无产阶级化及其结果：贫穷化［pauperization］）只是作为生产关系的阶级斗争的转化。而这种生产关系是能够被克服的，这意味着药的毒性是可以被消解的。相反，我认为药的毒性是永远不会被消解的。但是，它可以被打败（be fought）——这种斗争（combat）是知识的斗争。但现在谈这个问题还有点早，我们之后再来谈。

In the *Grundrisse*, the process of exteriorisation, as we shall see, is described in Marx's work *as grammatization*, that is, as a process of analytic formalization, discretization, reproduction and automation, as it is the case with tool machines in general, and as it will be systematically developed by Taylorism, particularly with the assembly line, this *grammatization* is not thought *as such*.

在《大纲》中，如我们所见，外化过程被马克思描述为*编程化*（*grammatization*），即一种分析的形式化、离散化（discretization）、再生产和自动化的过程，并且是在一般的工具机意义上而言的。这个过程将在泰罗制，特别是流水线中获得系统的发展，不过*编程化*还没有作出*同样*的思考。

Grammatization is a concept that comes from Sylvain Auroux, a french philosopher who is also a specialist of the history of sciences of language, and who used this word for describing how alphabetic writing appeared. But I use myself this concept of grammatization for describing how all the human movements and behaviours can be analysed, discretised and reproduced—and not only oral language, for example, gestures, as they are discretized and reproduced in a tool machine, or analog technologies of reproduction of perception, like photography, phonography, etc., or digital technologies, as they can reproduce the process of analytic understanding, for example, with big data or like Alphago. I will come back to this of course.

"编程化"这一概念来自席凡·欧胡（Sylvain Auroux）①，他是一位法国哲学家，也是一位语言学思想史家，他用这个概念来描述字母文字是如何出现的。但我用这个概念是为了描述一切人类运动和行为是如何被分析、离散和再生产的——不仅仅是口头语言，比如：姿势在工具机

---

① 席凡·欧胡（Sylvain Auroux, 1947— ）：法国哲学家、语言史学家，曾任法国里昂人文社会高等师范学院校长。其代表作有：《语法演化》（1994）、《语言哲学》（1996）等。——译者注

（tool machine）中被分解和再生产出来，或者模拟技术将感知再生产出来，如摄像、表音速记，等等，再比如数字技术能再生产分析的知性过程，比如利用大数据或像智能机器人 Alphago 所做的那样。我还会再谈这一点。

The process of grammatization is the process of exosomatisation and artificial reproduction of human noetic experience itself, that is, of the noetic experience, noetic meaning mental, this one become reproducible and then transmissible, that is, constituting a knowledge based on **an accumulation of tertiary retentions**. These recordings that are the result of grammatization are tertiary retentions indeed.

编程化过程就是外在化（exosomatisation）过程和人的智性经验本身的人为再生产，即智性经验、智性意义精神（noetic meaning mental）的人为再生产，这个过程变得可再生产和可传递，即建构一种建立在**第三持存积累**（**an accumulation of tertiary retentions**）之上的知识。这些作为编程化之结果的记录恰恰是第三持存。

But even though the *Grundrisse* describes the ***materialization of knowledge*** in the form of what I call tertiary retention, *the general question of knowledge in industrial society* *is not truly posed by dialectical materialism*: technics is not thematized as a *factor in knowledge as well as non-knowledge*, nor is there an *organology* of knowledge, or an *economy* of knowledge in the sense of a libidinal economy—of sublimated desire.

然而，尽管《大纲》是以我所说的第三持存的形式描述**知识的物化**(*materialization of knowledge*)，但工业社会中关于知识的一般问题并没有被辩证唯物主义真正提出来：技术（technics）没有被主题化（thematized）为*知识和非-知识*(*non-knowledge*)的一个要素，没有［提出］一种知识的*器官学*(an *organology* of knowledge)或力比多经济学——即升华的欲望（sublimated desire）意义上的一种知识*经济学*(an *economy* of knowledge)。

Here I must tell you that we need to connect Marx's philosophy with Freud's psychoanalytic theory of libidinal economy—if we agree to say that knowledge, as it is constituted by desire, as it was claimed by Socrates and Diotima in the *Symposium* is **always the result of a connection between the libidinal economy and the economy of exosomatisation that is production of goods in general**. And this connection must be formalized in the frame of the bio-economy that Nicholas

Georgescu-Roegen try to think with the concepts of entropy and exosomatisation.

这里，我必须指出，我们需要将马克思哲学与弗洛伊德的精神分析的力比多经济学理论联系起来。正如知识是由欲望构成的，正如苏格拉底和狄奥提玛在《会饮篇》中所主张的那样，如果我们同意知识**总是力比多经济和作为一般产品生产意义上的外在化经济（economy of exosomatisation）相联结的结果**，那么这种联结就必须在生命-经济学（bio-economy）的框架中加以形式化，生命-经济学就是尼古拉斯·乔治斯库-罗根（Nicholas Georgescu-Roegen）[①] 在《熵定律和经济过程》（*The Entropy Law and The Economic Process*）一书中试图用熵和外在化（exosomatisation）概念来建构的思想。

[①] 尼古拉斯·乔治斯库-罗根（Nicholas Georgescu-Roegen, 1906—1994）：美籍罗马尼亚经济学家、数学家和统计学家。最早将物理学原理（热力学定律和熵定律）应用于经济过程分析。其代表作有：《熵定律和经济过程》（1971）等。——译者注

**FORTH COURSE
30 MARCH 2016**
/
Reading Marx and Heidegger
in the Anthropocene
Technological épokhè,
Anthropocene and Neganthropocene

第 四 讲
2016.3.30
在人类纪阅读马克思和海德格尔:
技术中断、人类纪和逆人类纪

Proletarianization in and by digital tertiary retention is a *fact*. Is it **inevitable, and unavoidable?** Like Nicholas Carr, who suggests in the book *The Shallows*: *What the Internet is Doing to Our Brains*, Anderson claims, in his article on what he calls the end of theory, that is what I call myself the generalized proletarianization, that the destruction of attention is fatal. Nicholas Carr says the same in less joyful terms anyway.

居于数字第三持存并通过数字第三持存而进行的无产阶级化是一个事实。这个事实是**不可避免和无法预防**的吗？像尼古拉斯·卡尔（Nicholas Carr）① 在《浅薄：互联网如

---

① 尼古拉斯·卡尔（Nicholas Carr, 1959— ）：美国作家，《哈佛商业评论》前执行主编。其代表作有：《数字化企业》(2001)、《浅薄：互联网如何毒化了我们的大脑》(2010) 等。——译者注

何毒化了我们的大脑》（*The Shallows*：*What the Internet is Doing to Our Brains*）一书中所表明的，安德森在他的关于理论的终结即我所说的普遍的无产阶级化的那篇文章中宣称，注意力的破坏是灾难性的。尼古拉斯·卡尔则用不怎么令人愉快的说法表达了同样的观点。

I hold myself a **contrary** position—**The *fact of proletarianization* is *caused* by the digital, which, like *every* new form of tertiary retention, constitutes a new age of the *pharmakon*. It is inevitable that this *pharmakon* will have toxic effects if new therapies, new therapeutics, are not prescribed.**

而我持相反的观点：**就像*每一种*新的第三持存形式一样，由数字第三持*存*所产生的无产阶级化这个事实构成了*药*的新阶段。如果不能开出新的治疗方法（therapies）和治疗学（therapeutics），那么，这种*药*产生毒性效果将是不可避免的。**

Such prescriptions are the responsibility of the scientific world, the artistic world, the legal world, the world of the life of the spirit in general, and the world of citizens—and, in the first place, of those who claim to represent them. **Much courage** is required since it is a **struggle** that must face up against countless interests, **including those who partly suffer from this toxicity and partly feed off it.** This **period of suffering** constitutes **the stage of the chrysalis in a metamorphosis** we are now living everywhere in the world under the impact of the digital tertiary retention.

探寻新的治疗处方是科学界、艺术界、法律界、一般精神生活世界和市民世界——首先是市民代表——**的责任**。人们需要**很多勇气**：这是一场必须面对和反抗无数利益的斗争，其中既包括部分受这种毒性侵害的人们，也包括那些依赖这种毒性的人们。正是这段**痛苦时期**构成了**蛹的蜕变阶段**（the stage of the chrysalis in a metamorphosis）。而我们现在所生活世界的每一个角落都会受到数字第三持存的影响。

All new tertiary retention is and remain a *pharmakon* if it does not create *new transindividual arrangements* between **psychic and collective primary retentions and secondary retentions, and therefore between retentions and protentions** (expectations, through which objects of attention appear, and as such sources of **desire**)—which constitute **new attentional forms, new circuits of transindividuation, new meanings and new capabilities** of bringing about **the horizons of meaning that** are consistent. I say **new** transindividual arrangements because the new pharmakon that a new tertiary retention is appears in a society where **a *previous* pharmakon**, for example, printed alphabetic writing, had produced circuits of transindividuation and forms of attention based in.

一切第三持存是且仍旧是一种*药*（*pharmakon*），如果这种药不能在心理的和集体的原生持存和第二持存之间，因而在持存和前摄（即期望，注意对象通过期望而显现自身，欲望的来源同样如此）之间创造出*新的超个体安排*（*new transindividual arrangements*）——它构成了新的注意形式、新的超个体循环以及使意义域连贯一致的新的意义和能力。我说新超个体安排，是因为作为一种新第三持存的新药是出现在这样一种社会中，在那里，*以前的药*，比如印刷字母文字，已经产生了超个体化循环和以此为基础的注意形式。

Instead of creating ***new transindividual arrangements* between psychic and collective primary retentions and secondary retentions, the new *pharmakon* that digital tertiary retention is can on the contrary *substitute itself* for psychic and collective retentions insofar as the latter can produce significance and meaning *only* insofar as they are *individuated by* *all and shared* on the basis of psychic individuation processes, through processes of social transindividuation, that create relationships of solidarity, on which can be built, durably, and intergenerationally, *social systems*.

数字第三持存这种新*药*不是*在心理的和集体的原生持存和第二持存之间 创造出新的超个体安排*，相反，它*能取代心理的和集体的持存*，只要后者能产生意义（significance）和价值（meaning），*只要它们在通过社会个体化过程进行的心理个体化过程的基础上被所有人个体化和共享*。而社会个体化会创造出团结关系，并由此持久地、一代代地建立起*社会体系*（*social systems*）。

Last Monday, I told you that Bertrand Gille developed the concept of technical system for thinking the evolution of technics and technology. I now add that he showed how any technical system is always adjusting itself with what he called social systems, and we can represent this adjustment like this:

ST/SS

上周一，我说贝特兰·吉尔为了思考技术（technics）和工艺学（technology）的进化而发展了技术体系概念。我现在补充一下，他表明任何一种技术体系是如何总是随着社会体系来调整自身的。我们可以将这种调整表示为ST/SS。

Now, Bertrand Gilles shows also that：
现在，贝特兰·吉尔也表明：

1. During the history of technics, that is, of technical systems, and of the societies that, adjusted to theses technical systems, are constituted by social systems, there periods in which the adjusted technical system enters into a transformation, and changes into a new technical system.

1. 在技术史即技术体系史和社会史中，由社会体系构成的社会需要调整以适应技术体系，在某些阶段，调整过的技术体系会发生转变，变为一种新的技术体系。

2. During this change, it happens a disadjustment, that is the result of a change into the social systems that begins as troubles, conflicts and often revolutions or civil wars, or religious wars.

2. 在这种变化中，社会体系开始出现灾难、冲突，并经常发生革命、内战或宗教战争，从而导致一种失调

(disadjustment)。

3. Since the end of the eighteenth century, first in Europe, and then in America, and today everywhere in the world, the industrial technical system, based on technology, and not only technics, that is, based on scientific knowledge and mathematical formalisms, and not only on empirical experience, this industrial technical system is changing always faster, and always produces situations of disadjustment between the technical system and the social systems.

3. 自从18世纪末以来,那种发端于欧洲,进而是美国,直到今天遍布世界各地的工业技术体系(industrial technical system)是基于技术(technology),而不只是基于技艺(technics),也就是基于科学知识和数学形式主义,而不只是基于实证经验,这种工业技术体系总是变化得越来越快,总是在技术体系和社会体系之间产生失调状况。

A technical system is always based on what Bertrand Gilles calls a dominant technology—at the beginning of industrial revolution, the steam machine. Now, such a dominant technology is itself the result of a knowledge based on a hypomnesic tertiary retention, that supports and carriers it, and that is, in the case of the knowledge at the origin of the industrial revolution, the printed alphabetic writing, itself having made possible, after the Renaissance, the so-called Republic of Letters.

一种技术体系总是建立于贝特兰·吉尔所说的一种主导性技术（technology）之上——在工业革命早期是蒸汽机。现在，这种主导性技术是一种基于超级记忆第三持存的知识的产物，这种第三持存在工业革命早期的知识中就开始出现了，而印刷字母文字在文艺复兴之后就已经使所谓的文人共和国（Republic of Letters)① 成为可能。

Those **social systems**, that structure **collective individuals**, are themselves formed on the basis of **circuits of transindividuation**, themselves founded on knowledge and disciplines. Those knowledge and disciplines are what I call the therapeutics with which it is possible to take care of the new *pharmakon*, and, with such a <u>therapeutic use</u> of the *pharmakon*,

---

① "文人共和国（Republic of Letters，Respublica literaria）" 是指17世纪末到18世纪在欧美出现的远距离知识分子团体。它是启蒙时代不同国家和地区的知识分子以书信交流的方式穿越国界、打破语言文化隔阂而形成的一种形上共和国。书面文字和印刷术在其中发挥了重要作用，因为每个成员都是借助书信来交流思想、交换文章和小册子，并将扩大通信范围、吸收共同体成员视为己任。其中最著名的就是伏尔泰、卢梭、富兰克林和杰斐逊的书信往来，他们用书信搭建起一个横跨大西洋的文人共和国。——译者注

to *take care of the society*, and of people constituting such a society as psychic individuals and collective individuals.

那些建构**集体个人**的**社会体系**本身是建立在**超个体化的循环**，建立在知识和纪律之上的。那些知识和纪律就是我所说的疗法（**therapeutics**）。基于这种疗法，就有可能培养一种新*药*，按照这种*药*的<u>疗法用途</u>，就有可能*关照社会*和那些作为心理个人和集体个人而构成这个社会的人们。

*

What I described last Monday as a process of generalized proletarianization is the result of the disadjustment produced by the digital tertiary retention as it provokes what is called disruption.

上周一，我所说的普遍的无产阶级化过程是由数字第三持存引起的中断（disruption）所导致的失调造成的。

Disruption is the situation in which the speed of the evolution of technology is strategically exploited with the aim of creating gaps in the law and theoretical emptiness, which is a structural lack of knowledge. Digital tertiary retention thus creates a very specific state of proletarianization. Now, each type of hypomnesic pharmakon provokes such short-circuits, such a by-pass.

中断（disruption）是这样一种情境，技术（technology）的进化速度被策略性地用于这样的目的，即创造出规律和理论空白（即一种结构性的知识缺失）之间的间隙。因此，数字第三持存创造了一种非常特殊的无产阶级化状态。现在，每一种超级记忆的药（hypomnesic pharmakon）都会产生这种短路和绕道（by-pass）。

It is **always** possible for a *pharmakon* to **short-circuit and bypass** the circuits of transindividuation of which it is nevertheless the condition, and even though, **it is this *pharmakon* that makes it possible for psychic individuals, through their psychic retentions, to ex-press themselves, to form collective individuals founded on these traces and facilitation**, that is, on the secondary retentions and collective protentions emerging from this pharmacology. It is so because exosomatisation is the condition of noesis, of thought, of knowledge of every kind—savoir-vivre, how to live, savoir-faire, how to do, and conceptual or spiritual knowledge, how to think.

药使超个体化的循环发生**短路和绕道**总是可能的，尽管药是超个体化的条件，即使正是**药**使心理的个人通过他们的心理持存表达自己，形成集体的个人，后者（集体的个人）是建立于这些踪迹（traces）和便利（facilitation），建立于第二持存和出现于药理学中的集体前摄之上的。之所以这样，是因为外在化是认识（noesis）、思想和各种知识——如何生活的知识（savoir-vivre）、如何做事的知识（savoir-faire）以及如何思考的概念或思辨知识——的条件。

Generally, however, **a new *pharmakon* may start out by short-circuiting the psychosocial process. But the short-circuiting of psychic and collective individuation that is being caused today by automatized transindividuation processes, based on automation in real time and occurring on an immense scale, requires detailed analyses capable of taking account of the *remarkable novelty* of the digital *pharmakon*.**

然而，一般来说，一种新**药**可能是从使社会心理过程（psychosocial process）发生短路开始发挥作用的。但是，今天心理个体化和集体个体化的短路是基于实时地、大规模的自动化、通过自动化的超个体过程而发生的，这就要求**对这种数字化*药物*的*卓越新颖之处***（remarkable novelty of the digital *pharmakon*）进行思考和细致分析。

These analyses belong to what I call with the institute for research and innovation **digital studies**—that are not simply digital humanities, but **a new paradigm for all kinds of knowledge**, constituting **a new *episteme*** in the sense of Michel Foucault, requiring **new epistemologies** in the sense of Gaston Bachelard, and **belonging itself to** what I will describe in the next sessions of this seminar as what I call **general organology.**

这种分析就是我所说的研究与创新研究所的**数字化研究（digital studies）**——数字化研究不是简单的数字化人本主义，而是**一种面向所有知识的新范式**，它将建构一种米歇尔·福柯①意义上的**新*认识型*（new *episteme*）**，要求一种加斯通·巴什拉②意义上的**新认识论（new epistemologies）**，从而**属于**我将在下节课上说的**一般器官学（general organology）**。

---

① 米歇尔·福柯（Michel Foucault, 1926—1984）：法国当代著名哲学家。1950年，福柯毕业于巴黎高等师范学校。他在康吉莱姆的指导下，完成博士论文。1969年曾经任巴黎第八大学哲学系主任。1970年，他被任命为法国最有权威的学术体系，法兰西学院的思想体系史的教授。主要代表作：《疯癫与文明》（1961）、《临床医学的诞生》（1963）、《词与物》（1966）、《规训与惩罚》（1975）、《性史》（1976—1984）、《生命政治的诞生》（1978—1979）等。——译者注

② 加斯通·巴什拉（Gaston Bachelard 1884—1962）：法国哲学家、科学家、诗人。早年曾攻读自然科学，1927年获文学博士学位，1930年起先后任第戎大学、巴黎大学教授，1955年以名誉教授身份领导科学历史学院，并当选为伦理、政治科学院院士，1961年获法兰西文学国家大奖。主要代表作：《科学精神的形成》（1934）、《火的精神分析》（1938）、《水与梦：论物质的想象》（1942）、《空间的诗学》（1958）等。——译者注

*

To achieve socialization, that is, a collective individuation, **every new *pharmakon***—in this instance **a new form of tertiary retention**—always requires <u>the formation of *new knowledge*</u>, which always means **new therapies or therapeutics** for this new *pharmakon*, through which are constituted <u>**new ways of doing things and reasons to do things**</u>, to live and to think, that is, to **project consistencies**, which constitute at the same time **new forms of existence** and, ultimately, **new conditions of subsistence**.

为了实现社会化，即集体的个体化，**每一种新*药*——即一种新的第三持存形式**——总是需要<u>*新知识*的形成</u>（the formation of *new knowledge*），总是意味着关于这种新药的**新的疗法或治疗学**，由此建立<u>做事的新方式以及做事</u>、生活、思考即**筹划一致性**（project consistencies）的理性，这些同时构成了**新的存在形式**（new forms of existence），并最终构成**新的生存条件**（new conditions of subsistence）。

This **new knowledge** is the result of what I call **the second moment of an epokhal redoubling**—the *second moment of the*

TECHNOLOGICAL SHOCK that is always provoked whenever a new form of tertiary retention appears. Because of this second moment, I describe the technological change as it is accomplished a double epokhal redoubling.

这种新知识就是我所说的中断重复（epokhal redoubling）的第二环节的结果，即技术休克（TECHNOLOGICAL SHOCK）的第二环节的结果，后者总是在一种新的第三持存形式出现的时候被激活。因为这个第二环节，我把技术变革描述为它在完成一种二次中断重复（double epokhal redoubling）。

Claiming this, I affirm that technological change is always provoking
- an *épokhè* in the philosophical sense, that is, an interruption of belief and knowledge,

epokhal redoubling

a break in this knowledge that constituted the previous era, that is also what we call in history an epoch, a suspension of behavioural programs constituting the culture of such an epoch, and

double epokhal redoubling

· the reconstitution of new knowledge, new behaviours, new culture, new circuits of transindividuation and then new social systems, themselves constituting a new society.

为表明这一点,我要肯定技术变革总能激活:
·一个哲学意义上的*中断*(*épokhè*),即一种信仰和知识之间的断裂,一种与构成以前时代的知识的中断,这也就是我们所说的,一种构成一个历史时代的文化的行为程序(behavioural programs)的悬置。(即中断重复。)
·重建新知识、新行为、新文化以及新的超个体化循环,然后是重建新的社会体系,它们本身构成新的社会。(即二次中断重复。)

The problem, today, in what we call disruption, is that it seems impossible to reconstitute any knowledge, and that behaviours are now produced not by social systems, cultures and knowledge, but by marketing exploiting the big data and the digital tertiary retentions as they are **calculable, computable**, and as such constitute the **worldwide data economy.**

今天,我们所说的中断(disruption)问题在于似乎不可能重建任何知识，在于行为不是由社会体系、文化和知识生产出来，而是由利用大数据和数字第三持存的市场营销而生产出来，因为大数据和数字第三持存是**可计算的、可编程的**，并构成**全球性的数据经济**（worldwide data economy）。

Chris Anderson claims that the **contemporary fact of proletarianization** is insurmountable. I don't believe so. Anderson claims that, in what I just described as a **double epokhal redoubling**, with two moments, the one of the technological shock provoked by the new pharmakon and the one of the production of new knowledge during the second time of this **double** epokhal redoubling, **there is *no way* to bring about this *second moment*.**

克里斯·安德森（Chris Anderson）主张**当代无产阶级化的事实**是无法逾越的。我不这样认为。安德森认为，在我所说的**二次中断重复**（**double** epokhal redoubling）中有两个环节，一是由新药激起的技术休克（technological shock），二是在这种**二次**中断重复的第二阶段中生产新的知识，**而这第二个环节是无法实现的。**

But the reason of such a position lies in the fact that Chris Anderson himself happens to be **a businessman who** defends an ultra-liberal and <u>ultralibertarian</u> perspective. He remains faithful to the ultra-liberalism implemented in all industrial democracies after the **conservative revolution** that occurred at the beginning of the nineteen eighties, a "revolution" **that short-circuited processes of transindividuation via the analogue mass media, creating what Deleuze described as societies of control.**

但是,发生这种状况的原因是基于这样的事实,即克里斯·安德森自己就是一个为**超自由的和<u>超自由主义</u>(ultralibertarian)观点辩护的商人**。他仍然坚信 20 世纪 80 年代初出现的**保守主义革命**(conservative revolution)之后在所有工业民主国家实行的超自由主义(ultra-liberalism)。那是一场借助创造德勒兹所描述的控制社会的模拟大众传媒(analogue mass media)而使超个体化过程发生短路的"革命"。

*

In automatic society, those **digital networks that are referred to as "social" networks** channel such expressions by **submitting them to mandatory protocols to which psychic individuals bend because they are drawn to do so by the so-called** *network effect*, which, with the addition of social networking, becomes **an *automated herd effect*, that is, a highly mimetic situation**, and one that constitutes **a new form of *artificial crowd*** in the sense given to this phrase by Freud.

在自动社会中,那些被称为"社会"网络的数字网络引导着这样的表达,这些表达都屈从于强制规定,心理个人也屈从于这些强制规定,因为他们受到所谓的*网络影响*(*network effect*)而不得不这样做。再加上社会交际网络,这种影响就变成一种*自动的牧群效应*(*automated herd effect*),即一种高度模拟情境,而这种情境建构起一种弗洛伊德意义上的*乌合群众*(*artificial crowd*)的新形式。

Ten years ago, I compared TV or radio programs and channels to the constitution of **artificial and conventional crowds** such as they are analysed by Freud—for which he gives the examples of Army and Church. The **constitution of crowds**, and the conditions under which they can take shape, are the subjects of analyses by Gustave Le Bon, on which Freud commented at length:

The most striking peculiarity presented by a psychological crowd (in German: Masse) is the following. Whoever be the individuals that compose it, however like or unlike be their mode of life, their occupations, their characters, or their intelligence, the fact that they have been transformed into a crowd puts them in possession of a sort of collective mind which makes them feel, think, and act in a manner quite different from that in which each individual of them would feel, think, and act were he in a state of isolation. There are certain ideas and feelings that do not come into being, or do not transform themselves into acts except in the case of individuals forming a crowd.

The psychological crowd is a provisional being formed of heterogeneous elements, which for a moment are combined, exactly as the cells which constitute a living body form by their reunion a new being which displays characteristics very different from those possessed by each of the cells singly.

十年前，我曾将电视或广播节目与频道比作**乌合之众和普通群众**（**artificial and conventional crowds**）的构成，正如弗洛伊德也曾对他们做过分析——弗洛伊德给出的是军队和教会的例子。**群众的构成**（**constitution of crowds**）以及他们形成的条件，是古斯塔夫·勒庞（Gustave Le Bon）①的主要分析对象。对此，弗洛伊德做过详细论述：

> 一个心理群体（用德语说即大众［Masse］）的最显著特点在于，无论组成这个群体的个人是谁，无论他们的生活方式、职业、个性和智力是否相同，事实上，他们都已被带入一种群体，并拥有一种集体思想，从而使他们以一种与他们在孤立状态下可能采取的感受、思考和行动方式完全不同的方式进行感受、思考和行动。除非个人形成一个群体，否则，某些想法和感觉就不会显现出来，或者不会转变为行动。
>
> 心理群众是一种由各种要素形成的临时性存在，很像构成一个生命体的细胞，这些细胞通过聚合会形成一个新的存在，而这个新的存在会展现出每一单独的细胞所不具备的特性。

On the basis of the analyses by Le Bon, Freud showed that there are also "artificial" crowds, which he analyses through the examples of **the Church and the Army.**

---

① 古斯塔夫·勒庞（Gustave Le Bon，1841—1931）：法国社会心理学家、社会学家，群体心理学的创始人。其代表作有：《乌合之众：大众心理研究》（1895）等。——译者注

基于庞勒的这种分析，弗洛伊德表示也存在"乌合"之众，并借用**教会和军队**的例子进行了分析。

The **program industries** too, however, also form, every single day, and specifically through the **mass broadcast of programs**, such "artificial crowds." The latter become, as masses (and Freud refers precisely to *Massenpsychologie*—the psychology of masses), the permanent, everyday mode of being of the industrial democracies, which are at the same time what I call, in *Telecracie against democracy*, **industrial tele-cracies**.

然而，**编程产业**（**program industries**）每天特别通过**大众编程广播**（**mass broadcast of programs**）也塑造了这种"乌合之众"。后者作为大众（弗洛伊德所准确指认的*群众心理学*[*Massenpsychologie*, the psychology of masses]），成为工业民主制的永久的、日常的存在模式。这也是我在《远程统治反对民主》（*Telecracie against democracy*）这本书中所说的**工业远程-统治**（**industrial tele-cracies**）。

Generated by **digital tertiary retention**, net-connected artificial crowds constitute an economy of "crowd sourcing" that must be understood in manifold ways of which the so-called "cognitariat" would be one dimension. **Big data** is **one very large component** of those technologies that exploit the potential of crowd sourcing in its various forms, of which **social engineering** is a major element.

由数字第三持存产生的、由网络连接起来的乌合之众构成了一种"众包（crowd sourcing）"① 经济，我们必须从多个方面来理解它——其中，所谓的"知产阶级（cognitariat）"就是一个维度。**大数据**是那些以各种方式开发众包潜力的技术中的**一个非常大的组成部分**，其中社会工程（**social engineering**）是一个主要因素。

Through the **network effect**, through artificial crowds that the network effect allows to be created (such as the billions of psychic individuals who are now on Facebook), and through crowd sourcing that allows these crowds to be exploited, including through the use of big data, it is possible

- to **stimulate the production and auto-capture by**

---

① "众包"（Crowd Sourcing）概念最早由美国《连线》杂志记者杰夫·豪（Jeff Howe）于 2006 年 6 月提出。它的基本内涵是：一个公司或机构把过去由特定人员执行的工作任务，以自由自愿的形式外派给非特定的（通常是网络上的）大众的做法。实际上，"众包"概念是对互联网时代兴起的新型企业创新模式和商业模式的总结，它的最大特点就是充分利用网络资源，借助外部智慧，极大节约研发成本。参见：Jeff Howe (2008), *Crowdsourcing: Why the Power of the Crowd Is Driving the Future of Business*. New York: Crown Publishing Group. ——译者注

individuals of those tertiary retentions we call *personal data*, which spatialize their **psychosocial temporalities**;

• to **intervene**, by circulating this personal data **at the speed of light, in the processes of transindividuation** that are woven through circuits which are formed automatically and *performatively*;

• through these circuits, and **through the collective secondary retentions that form automatically, and no longer transindividually, to intervene in return, almost immediately, in psychic secondary retentions**, which is also to say, in protentions, expectations and, ultimately, in *personal behaviour*. It becomes possible **to *remotely control*, *to teleguide*, *one by one*, each of the members of a network**—this is what is referred to as "personalization."

借助网络效应（network effect）所创造出来的乌合之众（比如现在活跃在脸书上的几十亿心理个人），通过使乌合之众得以被利用的众包，包括使用大数据，以下这些情况将成为可能：

• 通过那些我们称为*个人数据*(*personal data*) **第三持存的个人**来促进生产和自动-获取（auto-capture），这些个人数据使他们的社会心理时间（psychosocial temporalities）空间化；

・通过使个人数据**以光速传播来干预超个体化过程**，这个过程迂回穿过那些自动地、*述行地*（*performatively*）形成的循环；

・通过这些循环，通过**自动地、而不是超个体化地形成的集体第二持存，反过来干预，几乎是直接地干预心理的第二持存**，也就是说，干预前摄、期望，并最终干预个人行为（*personal behaviour*）。这样对**网络中的各个成员进行一个个地远程控制**（remotely control）**和远程指导**（tele-guide）就成为可能——这就是所说的"人格化（personalization）"。

The **internet is a *pharmakon*** that can thus become a technique for **hyper-control and social dis-integration. Unless there is a new politics of individuation**, that is, unless **attention is formed through the specific tertiary retentions** that make possible a new technical milieu（and every associated milieu, beginning with language）, it will inevitably become a cause of **dissociation**.

因特网是一种*药*，这种药将会成为一种实现超级控制（hyper-control）和社会瓦解（social dis-integration）的技术（technique）。除非有一种新的**个体化政治学**（politics of individuation），即除非**通过有可能产生新的技术环境（和以**

语言为开端的每一相关环境）的**特殊的第三持存而形成（新的）注意力**，否则，因特网将不可避免地成为一种导致**分解**（dissociation）的诱因。

*

The hyper-industrial situation takes what Deleuze called **societies of control**, founded on modulation by the mass media, to a stage of **hyper-control** generated by **self-produced personal data, self-collected and self-published by people themselves**—whether **knowingly or otherwise**—and exploited by applying high-performance computing to these massive data sets.

超级工业情境使德勒兹所说的建立于大众传媒调节之上的**控制社会**进入**超级控制**阶段，这种超级控制产生于**大众对个人数据的自我生产、自我收集和自我发布**——无论这些行为是**有意还是无意**——并通过对这些大量数据集进行高性能计算而加以利用。

This *automatized modulation* establishes what Thomas Berns and Antoinette Rouvroy have called **algorithmic governmentality**.

这种*自动化调节*(*automatized modulation*)建立了托马斯·伯恩斯(Thomas Berns)和安托瓦内特·鲁弗鲁(Antoinette Rouvroy)所说的*算法治理*(**algorithmic governmentality**)。

The **digital** allows **all technological automatisms to be unified**(mechanical, electromechanical, photo-electrical, electronic, and so on), by **implanting the producer into the consumer** and through the production of all manner of **sensors, actuators and related software**. But the truly unprecedented aspect of digital unification is that it allows **articulations *between* ALL THESE AUTOMATISMS: TECHNOLOGICAL, SOCIAL, PSYCHIC AND BIOLOGICAL**—and this is the main point of **neuro-marketing** and neuro-economics. This integration, however, leads inevitably to **TOTAL AUTOMATISATION**, but **it is not just public authority, social and educational systems, intergenerational relations and psychic structures that find themselves disintegrated**—for **mass markets** to be formed, and for **all the *commodities* secreted by the consumerist system to be absorbed, wages** needed to be distributed so as **to supply purchasing power**, but <u>it is this very economic system that has disintegrated and that is becoming *functionally insolvent*</u>.

这种**数字化**通过**将生产者置入消费者**,通过生产各种**传感器、执行器和相关软件**,就能够使一切技术自动主义统一起来(机械的、电机的、光电的、电子的,等等)。但数字一体化的真正的前所未有的方面在于,它能够使所有**这些自动主义**之间**相互接合:技术的、社会的、心理的、生物的自动主义**——这就是神经-市场学(neuro-marketing)和神经-经济学(neuro-economics)的主要方面。这种一体化必然导致总体的自动化(TOTAL AUTOMATISATION),但是,包括公共权威、社会和教育体系、代际关系和心理结构等领域都发现它们自身的分裂(disintegrated):因为大众市场要形成,因为一切*商品*都被消费体系所吸纳和掩盖起来,工资要发放以支持购买力。<u>正是这样的经济体系已经发生分裂,而且正在*功能上*变得破产</u>。

*

The **PHARMACOLOGICAL CHARACTER of the digital age** has become more or less clear to those who belong to it, resulting in what I am calling **"net blues"** —particularly after Edward Snowden revelations, and also with the increasing of social networking based on Facebook's strategy to exploit the **network effect** in order **to shortcircuit the web**: the **state of fact** constituted by this new age of tertiary retention **HAS**

FAILED TO PROVIDE A NEW STATE OF LAW. *On the contrary*, it has **liquidated the rule of law** as produced by the retentional systems of the bygone epoch. **Property law**, for example, has been directly challenged by activists through their practices in relation to **free software**, and through reflecting on the "commons" —including some young artists who are attempting to devise a new economic and political framework for their thinking. But thus was never concretized by a new state of law.

数字化时代的药理学特征（PHARMACOLOGICAL CHARACTER）对于那些附属于它的人们来说已经变得或多或少清楚了，结果就是我所说的"**网络蓝调（net blues）**"——特别是在爱德华·斯诺登（Edward Snowden）事件曝光之后，这也是伴随着由于脸书利用**网络影响（network effect）**来使网络发生短路的策略所导致的社交网络的增长而产生的：由这种新的第三持存时代所构成的**事实状况还没有提供一种新的法律状况**。*相反地*，它已**清除了**过去时代的持存体系所产生的**法律规则**。比如，**财产法**已经直接遭到了那些通过关于**免费软件**的实践、通过对"大同世界（commons）"的设想的行动者——包括一些尝试制定新的经济和政治框架来思考的年轻艺术家们的挑战。然而，这还从未被一种新的法律状况所具体化。

These questions must, however, be seen as part of **an *epistemic* and *epistemological* transition from fact to law**, and by canonical reference to **apodictic** experience—projecting law **beyond** fact. The **passage from fact to law** is firstly a matter of **discovering** *in facts* the *necessity of* **INTERPRETING** *them*, that is, of projecting **beyond** *the facts* themselves, but also *on the basis of facts* **that are not themselves self-sufficient**—onto **another plane** towards which they beckon: that of a **consistence** through which and in which we must "believe" (and here I use words used by Deleuze in *The Time-Image*).

然而，这些问题必须被看作一种**从事实到规律的*认识的*和*认识论的*变革**的一部分，这种变革是通过对**必然经验**——即**超越**事实的规律投射——的经典参考而实现的。从事实向规律的过程首先是*在这些事实中发现解释它们的必然性*，即在**事实本身**之外进行投射，但这也是*基于那些不能自足的事实之上*——基于它们被引向**另一种境界**（another plane）：它是我们必须"相信"和穿越的一种一致性（这里我用德勒兹的话说就是*时间-图像*〔*Time-Image*〕）。

This other plane is the one of **negentropy**.

Negentropy is an object of belief because it is the improbable possibility of a bifurcation—improbable because not calculable. On the contrary, systems of computation are structurally entropic, this means, toxic. So, a pharmakon, as a product of exosomatisation, always opens two opposite possibilities entropic possibilities, that are toxic possibilities, and negentropic possibilities, that are capable to inscribe a bifurcation in the becoming, such a bifurcation transforming becoming into future—and I will try to show you later how it is possible and necessary to refer to Heidegger in order to think this difference between future and becoming, but also why we must overcome Heidegger and the ontological difference on which this notion of protention this is future is based, and to introduce the questions of exosomatisation and negentropy in his existential analytic.

这另一种境界就是一种**负熵**（**negentropy**）。

负熵是一种信仰对象，因为它是一个分叉点的不大可能的可能性——不可能是因为它不可计算。相反，计算系统在结构上是熵的，这意味着它是有毒的。所以，一种药，作为外在化的产物，总是有两种相反的可能性：熵的可能性和负熵的可能性，前者是有毒的可能性，后者则能在生成中产生一个分叉点（bifurcation），这个分叉点会将生成转化为未来——之后我将说明这是何以可能的，并且有必要参考海德格尔来思考未来（future）和生成（becoming）

的不同，但同时我们必须克服海德格尔和作为前摄或未来之基础的本体论差异，介绍他的存在论分析中关于外在化和负熵的问题。

We will see also that from such a point of view, it is possible and necessary to reinterpret what Heidegger called Gestell, Bestand and Ereignis.

从这一观点出发，我们也将会看到，重新解释海德格尔的座架（Gestell），持存（Bestand）和生成（Ereignis）概念是可能的和必要的。

If we are now living in the **Anthropocene**, this state of fact is not sustainable: we must pass to a state of law in which negentropy becomes the criterion of all types of value, the value of value, and this is why we must enter into the

NEGANTHROPOCENE.

如果我们现在生活在**人类纪**，这种事实状况就不是可持续的：我们必须进入一种规律状况，在其中负熵成为一切价值的标准，成为价值的价值，这就是我们为什么必须进入**逆人类纪**（**NEGANTHROPOCENE**）。

The **context** of this task of thinking conceived as therapeutic is one in which **automatisms** of all kinds are being technologically integrated by digital automatisms. **The unique and very specific aspect of this situation is the way that digital tertiary retention succeeds in totally rearranging assemblages or montages of psychic and collective retentions and protentions.** The challenge is **to invert this situation** towards **a new idea of dis-automatization that would arise from out of today's dis-integrating automatization.** And this is the stake of my contemporary reading of the *Grundrisse*—but we will see that later.

这种被看作是治疗性的思想任务的**语境**就是，在其中，各种各样的**自动主义**都在技术上被数字化自动主义一体化了。**这种情境的独特而非常特殊的方面就在于，那种使数字第三持存成功地在总体上重新排列心理的和集体的持存以及前摄的集合或剪辑的方式。**而挑战则在于**将这种情境翻转为一种从今天非一体性的自动化（dis-integrating automatization）中产生出来的非自动化（dis-automatization）的新思想**。这就是我对《大纲》进行当代解读的关键点——之后我们将会谈到这一点。

**FIFTH COURSE
6 APRIL 2016**
/
Organology, Economy and Ecology

第 五 讲
2016.4.6
器官学、经济学和生态学

Today, we will begin to address **questions coming from Heidegger,** in order **to understand better the previously questions we asked with Marx.** And this will permit us to take into account **the urgent question of ecology** in the age of the **absolutely computational** capitalism.

今天，我们开始讨论**海德格尔提出的问题**，以便更好地理解我们之前向马克思提出的问题。这让我们有可能对在**完全计算机化**（absolutely computational）的资本主义时代中出现的刻不容缓的生态学问题（the urgent question of ecology）进行思考。

1. Ecology, organology, cosmology
生态学、器官学、宇宙学

In *A Thousand Ecologies*: *The Process of Cyberneticization and General Ecology*①, **Erich Hörl** takes up a proposition wherein the French poet **Michel Deguy**, who is also a philosopher, makes **ecology the "task of thinking"**. And he points out that a phrase such as **the "task of thinking"** owes something to **Martin Heidegger**. On the basis of this remark, he explains why **Heidegger could not himself assume such an ("ecological") task** *in our epoch*, that is, **inasmuch as** it posits that *humanity's ecological dimension of humanity is what, above all, today reveals its primordially artificial*

---

① Erich Hörl (2013) A Thousand Ecologies: The Process of Cyberneticization and General Ecology. IN: Diedrich Diederichsen and Anselm Franke (eds.) *The Whole Earth*: *California and the Disappearance of the Outside*. Berlin: Sternberg Press, pp. 121 – 130.

constitution—and its "artifacticity".①

在《一千种生态学：赛博化过程和一般生态学》②一书中，**埃里希·霍尔（Erich Hörl）**③ 提到法国诗人和哲学家**米歇尔·德居（Michel Deguy）**④ 将生态学看作"**思考的任务**"（task of thinking）。他指出，"思考的任务（task of thinking）"这一提法在某种意义上要归功于**马丁·海德格尔**。由此，他就解释了为什么**海德格尔不能设想**我们时代

---

① Ibid., p. 122: "Contrary to all of the ecological preconceptions that bind ecology and nature together, ecology is increasingly proving to epitomize the un- or non-natural configuration that has been established over more—than half a century by the extensive cyberneticization and computerization of life. The radical technological mediation that has been implemented since 1950 through the process of cyberneticization—and which today operates within the sensory and intelligent environments that exist in micro-temporal realms, in pervasive media and ubiquitous computing—causes **the problem of mediation as such to come fully into focus,** exposing it with a radicality never seen before. As such, it is both **a problem and question of constitutive relationality**; or, more precisely—to paraphrase Gilbert Simondon—the problem of **an original relationship between the individual and its milieu, with which it has always already been coupled and which would not simply constitute a ready-made, prior 'natural' environment** to which it would have had to adapt, but **which must rather be conceived as the site of its originary and inescapable artifacticity,** with which it is conjoined…"

② Erich Hörl（2013）A Thousand Ecologies: The Process of Cyberneticization and General Ecology. IN: Diedrich Diederichsen and Anselm Franke（eds.）*The Whole Earth: California and the Disappearance of the Outside.* Berlin: Sternberg Press, pp. 121 – 130.

③ 埃里希·霍尔（Erich Hörl，1967— ）：奥地利哲学家与文化理论家，德国吕讷堡大学文化批判研究院副院长，吕讷堡大学文化与数字媒体美学研究所（ICAM）教授、数字文化研究实验室高级研究员，曾任德国鲁尔大学媒体技术哲学教授、包豪斯大学文化科技与媒体哲学研究员。其代表作有：《技术条件》（2011）、《一千种生态学：赛博化过程和一般生态学》（2013）等。——译者注

④ 米歇尔·德居（Michel Deguy，1930— ）：法国诗人、诗歌批评家、哲学家。曾任国际哲学学院院长（1989—1992），现任巴黎第八大学教授。其代表作有：《诗集：1960—1970》（1973）、《浮雕》（1975）等。——译者注

的这种（生态学的）任务，这是因为它假设了*人的*人类生态学维度首先是今天所揭示的原真性的人为构成——和它的"人为性（artifacticity）"。①

Furthermore, Erich Hörl himself refers to Gilbert **Simondon** to show that, in addition to the fertility of the terms and analyses proposed by **this thinker of relation**, <u>ecology</u>, insofar as it is above all a **relational form of thinking**, must be conceived **starting from cybernetics and from Simondon's critique thereof**（in the Kantian sense of "critique"）, and by **taking up this program on new bases（other than those of Norbert Wiener）**.

而且，埃里希·霍尔提到吉尔伯特·西蒙栋（Gilbert Simondon）时指出，除了**这个思想家在关系问题上提出了丰富的术语和分析之外**，（他还指出）只要<u>生态学</u>首先是一种关

---

① 同上页②，第122页："与所有将生态学和自然绑在一起的生态学偏见不同，**生态学越来越被证明是一种非自然性结构的典范，这种结构已经被生活的普遍赛博化和计算机化建构了半个多世纪。自1950年以来，激进的技术调解已经通过赛博化过程来加以实施**——今天它则是在遍布微观-时间领域、无处不在的大众传媒和计算机信息中的感官环境和智力环境中进行的——这使得具有前所未有的**彻底性的调解问题成为广泛关注的焦点**。这样一来，它就既是一个本质**关系性**（**constitutive relationality**）的难题，又是一个本质**关系性**的问题。更准确地说——借用西蒙栋的话来说——就是一个关于**个人与他的环境的原始关系**的难题。个人总是与这种**环境**结合在一起，而这种环境不是简单地构成一种现成的、先于'自然'环境的、不得不去适应的**环境**，相反，它必须被看作一种个人的原始的、不可避免的人为场域……"

系性的思考形式，那么就必须从控制论（cybernetics）和西蒙栋对控制论的批判（康德意义上的"批判"）入手来思考它，并把这个问题放在新的平台（除了诺伯特·维纳 [Norbert Wiener] 的观点）上进行思考。

This is what leads Hörl to conceive of **a general ecology capable of assuming the task of thinking on the basis of a techno-logical perspective in which** **cybernetics**, which was for Heidegger, too, **the science characteristic of "modern technics"** (see "*Zeit und Sein*"), **constitutes the new conceptual framework that opens the way for a new "encyclopedism" in Simondon's sense**—forming **the new horizon of the transindividual** (which in Simondon constitutes meaning) insofar as **it bears the promise of a reconciliation between "culture" and technics.**

这就引导霍尔去思考一种能够将思考的任务设定在技术-逻辑视角基础上的一般生态学。在这种技术-逻辑视角中，**控制论**，即对海德格尔来说的"**现代技术**"的科学控制论（参见《时间与存在》[*Zeit und Sein*]），构成了一种新的概念框架，为通向一种西蒙栋意义上的新的"百科全书（encyclopedism）"开辟了道路——形成（西蒙栋赋予的意义上的）超个体的新视域，因为它承载着在"**文化**"**和技术之间建立一种协调**（reconciliation）的希望。

第五讲
137

I have myself argued for ten years that **cybernetics** must be understood as **the most recent stage of a process of grammatization**—a question I addressed in the previous session of this seminar—that can be thought only **through the perspective that I call a "general organology"**, which I believe to be a more apt way of approaching these questions than through what Simondon himself called in the book *Du mode d'existence des objets techniques* a "mechanology" (although he did occasionally use the term "organology").①

十年来我始终认为，**控制论**必须被理解为**编程化（grammatization）过程的最新阶段**——这是我在以前的系列研讨课上提出的一个问题——这只能**从我所说的"一般器官学"的角度**进行思考。我认为，在这些问题上，这是比西蒙栋在《技术客体的存在方式》（*Du mode d'existence des objets techniques*）这本书中提出的"机械学（mechanology）"（尽管他也偶尔使用"器官学"这个术语②）更合适的路径。

General organology, that use Bertrand Gille's concepts of

---

① For example, in Gilbert Simondon (2010) *Communication et information: Cours et conférences*. Chatou: Éditions de la transparence, p. 167.

② For example, in Gilbert Simondon (2010) *Communication et information: Cours et conférences*. Chatou: Éditions de la transparence, p. 167.

technical system and of social systems we saw last week, is a **method of thinking, at one and the same time, technical, social and psychic becoming,** where technical becoming must be thought via the concept of the **technical system,** as it adjusts and is adjusted to **social systems,**

TS/SS

themselves constituted by **psychic apparatuses,** that is, by psychic individuals. We saw that a technical system like the one based on **network engineering** can also short-circuit social systems and then psychic individuals.

借用上周我们已经看到的贝特兰·吉尔（Bertrand Gille）关于技术体系和社会体系的概念来说，**一般器官学就是一种思维方法**，同时也是**技术的、社会的和心理的生成**，其中技术的生成必须借助**技术体系**这个概念来加以思考，因为**技术体系**（TS）调整**社会体系**（SS），同时又被社会体系所调整，而社会体系本身又是由**心理器官**（psychic apparatuses）即心理的个人所构成的。我们看到，一种技术体系就像一种以**网络工程**（network engineering）为基础的系统一样，也能使社会体系和心理个人发生短路。

We also saw last week that there is no human society

that is not constituted by a technical system. A technical system is traversed by **evolutionary tendencies** that, when they concretely express themselves, induce a **change in the technical system.**

上周我们也提到，没有哪个人类社会不是由一种技术体系构成的。技术体系被**进化趋势**所超越，这种进化趋势包含着**技术体系本身的变革。**

Such a change necessitates **adjustments** with the other systems constituting society—those systems that Bertrand Gille called social systems in a sense that should be specified in confrontation with **Niklas Luhmann.**

这种变革必然**调节**了构成社会的其他系统——贝特兰·吉尔所说的社会系统在某种意义是与**尼克拉斯·卢曼**（**Niklas Luhmann**）不同的。

These **adjustments** constitute **a suspension and a re-elaboration of the socio-ethnic programs or socio-political programs** that form the unity of the social body. This re-elaboration, that I called in the previous sessions the double epokal redoubling,

double
epokhal
redoubling

is **a selection amongst possibilities**, effected across what I call **retentional systems**, themselves constituted by mnemo-techniques or mnemo-technologies that are **hypomnesic tertiary retentions**, the **becoming** of which is **tied to** that **of the technical system**, and the **appropriation of** which permits the elaboration of **selection criteria constituting a motive**, that is, **a characteristic stage of psychic and collective individuation.**

这些**调**节构成一种塑造社会体统一性的**社会-民族计划或社会-政治计划的悬停和再-细化（re-elaboration）**。这种再-细化就是我之前所说的二次中断重复，它是对影响整个**持存系统（retentional systems）的众多可能性之中的一种选择**。这些持存系统本身是由作为**超级记忆第三持存**的记忆-技能（mnemo-techniques）或记忆-技术（mnemo-technologies）构成的，而超级记忆第三持存的**生成**是**与技术体系的生成联系在一起的**，对超级记忆技术的占用使对构成心理的和集体的**一个典型阶段或动机的选择标准**进行细化成为可能。

Here, I must reintroduce the theme of **exosomatisation**,

that is the core of Georgescu-Roegen's conception of economy. In several papers and lectures he gave, Georgescu-Roegen (*pour une révolution bioéconomique*) showed that **the question opened by the exosomatic form of life that is human life is the criteria of selection in this exosomatic becoming** of the artificial organogenesis that human evolution is. Such a selection is an artificial one, and here, we should revisit Engels and Marx's definition of ideology as well as of class struggle form such a point of view.

这里，我必须重新介绍一下**外在化**这个主题，它是乔治斯库-罗根（Georgescu-Roegen）经济学概念的核心。在他的几篇文章和演讲中，他（在《生物经济学革命》[*pour une révolution bioéconomique*]① 中）指出，**生命的外在化形式提出了这样的问题，即人类生活是人造器官形成即人类进化的外在化生成的选择标准**。这种选择是一种人为选择，这里我们需要从这个角度出发来重新回顾一下马克思与恩格斯对意识形态和阶级斗争的定义。

I claim that **such a selection is overdetermined by the hypomnesic tertiary retentions** that are the fruits of the process

---

① 参见 Antoine Missemer（2013）*Nicholas Georgescu-Roegen, pour une révolution bioéconomique*. Lyon: ENS Éditions. ——译者注

of grammatization wherein all the fluxes or flows [*flux*] through which symbolic and existential acts are linked can be **discretized, formalized and reproduced.** The most well-known of these processes is written language and **digital tertiary retention** is the most recent of these processes.

我认为，<u>这种选择是由超级记忆第三持存所过度决定的</u>，后者是**编程化**过程的结果。在这个过程中，一切使象征性行为和存在性行为联系起来的流动（fluxes or flows [*flux*]）能够被**离散化、形式化和再生产**。其中最显著的过程就是最新出现的书面语言（written language）和**数字第三持存**（digital tertiary retention）。

General organology defines the **rules for analysing, thinking and prescribing human facts at three parallel but indissociable levels** of the **psychosomatic**, which is the **endosomatic** level, the **artifactual**, which is the **exosomatic** level, and the **social**, which is the **organisational** level. It is an analysis of the relations between **organic organs, technical organs and social organisations.**

一般器官学从三个平行但不可分离的层面定义了分析、思考和规划人类事实的规则，这三个层面即心理的即体内的层面（endosomatic level）、人造的即体外的层面和社会的即**组织**的层面。这是一种对**有机器官、技术器官和社会组织**之间关系的分析。

Those social organisations are social systems that define and prescribe, as therapeutics of the pharmaka that compose the technical system, and that are knowledge, criteria of artificial selections into the possibilities of evolution opened by the last stage of exosomatisation, that is, by the last stage of individuation of the technical system, as it is also a double epokhal redoubling.

这些社会组织就是对构成技术体系的药的诸疗法进行定义和规定的各种社会体系，这些疗法就是知识，就是对进化的各种可能性进行人为选择的标准。而这种进化的诸可能性是由外在化的最后阶段，即技术体系的个体化的最后阶段所打开的，因为它也是一种二次中断重复（double epokhal redoubling）。

Prescription of such criteria is called **politics**. Marx showed that **such a politics is also and first of all a political economy**, in which a conflict is always at work, and that is today capitalism based on a process of grammatization. Marx described this grammatization in the *Grundrisse*.

Labour is the necessary tendency of capital, as we have seen. The transformation of the means of labour into machinery is the realization of this tendency. **In machinery, objectified labour materially confronts living labour as a ruling power** and as an active subsumption of the latter under itself, not only by appropriating it, but in the real production process itself; the relation of capital as value which appropriates value-creating activity is, in fixed capital existing as machinery, posited at the same time as the relation of the use value of capital to the use value of labour capacity; further, **the value objectified in machinery appears as a presupposition against which the value-creating power of the individual labour capacity is an infinitesimal, vanishing magnitude; the production in enormous mass quantities which is posited with machinery destroys every connection of the product with the direct need of the producer, and hence with direct use value;** it is already posited in the form of the product's production and in the relations in which it is produced that it is produced only as a conveyor of value, and its use value only as condition to that end. **In machinery, objectified labour itself appears not only in the form of product or of the product employed as means of labour, but in the form of the force of production itself. The development of the means of labour into machinery is not an accidental moment of capital, but is rather the historical reshaping of the traditional, inherited means of labour into a form adequate to capital.**

As an exteriorisation or externalisation of knowledge into automata, you can see here why knowledge cannot be thought today if such a thought is not capable to understand what is a tertiary retention.

The accumulation of knowledge and of skill, of the general productive forces of the social brain, is thus absorbed into capital, as opposed to labour, and hence appears as an attribute of capital, and more specifically of *fixed capital*, in so far as it enters into the production process as a means of production proper. *Machinery* appears, then, as the most ade-

quate form of *fixed capital*, and fixed capital, in so far as capital's relations with itself are concerned, appears as *the most adequate form of capital* as such. In another respect, however, in so far as fixed capital is condemned to an existence within the confines of a specific use value, it does not correspond to the concept of capital, which, as value, is indifferent to every specific form of use value, and can adopt or shed any of them as equivalent incarnations. In this respect, as regards capital's external relations, it is *circulating capital* which appears as the adequate form of capital, and not fixed capital.

Further, in so far as **machinery develops with the accumulation of society's science**, of productive force generally, **general social labour presents itself not in labour but in capital.** The productive force of society is measured in *fixed capital*, exists there in its objective form; and, inversely, the productive force of capital grows with this general progress, which capital appropriates free of charge. This is not the place to go into the development of machinery in that is also called here the fixed capital.

这种标准的处方被称为**政治学**，马克思指出**这种政治学首先是一种政治经济学**，其中冲突总是存在，这就是今天建立在一种编程化过程之上的资本主义。在《大纲》(*Grundrisse*) 中，马克思将编程化描述为知识外化或客观化进入自动机器，即：

> 提高劳动生产力和最大限度否定必要劳动，正如我们已经看到的，是资本的必然趋势。劳动资料转变为机器体系，就是这一趋势的实现。在机器体系中，对象化劳动在物质上与活劳动相对立而成为支配活劳动的力量，并主动地使活劳动从属于自己，这不仅是通过对活劳动的占有，而且是在现实的生产过程中实现的。在作为机器体系存在的固定资本中，资本作为把创造价值的活动占为己有的价值这样一种关系，同时表现为资本的使用价值与劳动能力的使用价值的关系。
>
> 其次，对象化在机器体系中的价值表现为这样一个前提，即同它相比，单个劳动能力创造价值的力量作为无限小的量而趋于消失。由于机器体系所造成的规模巨大的生产，产品同生产者的直接需要的任何联系也都消失了，从而同直接使用价值的任何联系也都消失了。产品生产的形式和产品生产的关系已经意味着：产品只是作为价

值的承担者被生产出来，而它的使用价值只是实现这一目的的条件。在机器[体系]中，对象化劳动本身不仅直接以产品的形式或者以当作劳动资料来使用的产品的形式出现，而且以生产力本身的形式出现。劳动资料发展为机器体系，对资本来说并不是偶然的，而是使传统的继承下来的劳动资料适合于资本要求的历史性变革。①

在这里你们就会明白，为什么今天知识无法被思考，如果这种思想不能理解什么是第三持存。在《大纲》中，这种第三持存也被称为固定资本。即：

> 知识和技能的积累，社会智力的一般生产力的积累，与劳动相对立而被吸收在资本当中，从而表现为资本的属性，更明确些说，只要后者作为真正的生产资料加入生产过程，它便表现为固定资本的属性。因此，机器体系表现为固定资本的最合适的形式，而固定资本——就资本对自身的关系来看——则表现为资本一般的最适当的形式。另一方面，就固定资本被束缚在自己一定的使用价值的存在中这一点来看，它是不符合资本的概念的，

---

① 参见《马克思恩格斯全集》第 31 卷，人民出版社，1998 年版，第 92 页。——译者注

因为作为价值来说,资本采取任何特定的使用价值形式都是无所谓的,它可以把任何一种使用价值形式作为自己一视同仁的化身来加以采用或者抛弃。从这方面来看,就资本对外部的关系而言,流动资本同固定资本相比表现为资本的适当形式。

其次,从机器体系随着社会知识的积累、整个生产力的积累而发展来说,代表一般社会劳动的不是劳动,而是资本。社会的生产力是用固定资本来衡量的,它以物的形式存在于固定资本中,另一方面,资本的生产力又随着资本无偿占有的这种普遍的进步而得到发展。这里无须详细地研究机器体系的发展。①

Nevertheless, we will soon see that Marx himself forgets or lacks this question in *Das Kapital* when he writes about the difference between a bee and an architect. We will go back to these questions later of course.

尽管如此,我们马上会发现,当马克思自己在《资本论》中写到蜜蜂和建筑师之间的区别时,他忘记或忽视了这一问题。我们将会在以后的课上回到这个问题。

---

① 参见《马克思恩格斯全集》第 31 卷,人民出版社,1998 年版,第 92—93 页。——译者注

*

As **it is always possible for the <u>arrangements between the psychosomatic and artifactual organs</u>** to become toxic and destructive for the organic organs, <u>**general organology is a pharmacology**</u>. Now, today we must project these perspectives into a broader, more encompassing, more clearly urgent and "relevant" (as we say in English) consideration of what for the last sixteen years, since Paul Krutzen statement, has been referred to as the **Anthropocene**, which I would like to consider from the point of view of what I provisionally call, with regard to Alfred North Whitehead, a "**speculative cosmology**".

由于<u>心理器官和人造器官之间的安排</u>总有可能对有机器官变得具有毒性和破坏性,因此<u>一般器官学就是一种药理学</u>。现在,我们必须将这些观点投向一种更加宽广、更具包含性、更显迫切和"紧要"的谓之**人类纪**的思考中。

这一努力自保罗·克鲁岑（Paul Krutzen）① 提出以来已经十六年了。我想从与阿尔弗雷德·诺思·怀特海（Alfred North Whitehead）有关的暂时称之为"**思辨宇宙学（speculative cosmology）**"的角度来思考人类纪问题。

The speculativity of such a cosmology, which would also be **performative**, leads to the theoretical and practical prospect and program of **a passage from the Anthropocene to what I propose naming the Neganthropocene,**

Neganthropocene

all these issues being placed **in the context of the cosmological stakes of thermodynamics**, with the notion of **entropy** that is its second law, **and of the analysis of life *and technics* as negentropic inversions and bifurcations** that nevertheless **do not oppose entropy but divert it,** *by deferring it*, in a process resembling what Derrida, in this text I have sent in an English

---

① 保罗·约瑟夫·克鲁岑（Paul Jozef Crutzen, 1933— ）：荷兰大气化学家，1995 年诺贝尔化学奖得主，德国马克斯-普朗克化学研究所大气化学部主任。2000 年，他与尤金·F. 施特默（Eugene F. Stoermer）在《国际地圈生物圈计划通讯》（IGBP Newsletter）第 41 期正式提出"人类纪"概念：强调自 1784 年瓦特发明蒸汽机以来，人类的作用越来越成为一个重要的地质营力。随着他在《自然》杂志 2002 年第 415 期上发表《人类地质学》（*Geology of Mankind*）一文，继续阐发关于人类纪的观点，这一概念已得到学术界和科学媒体界的普遍接受，并产生深远影响。参见 Crutzen, P. J. & Stoermer, E. F. (2002) **The "Anthropocene"**. *IGBP Newsletter*, 41: 17-18. 与 Crutzen, P. J. (2002) **Geology of mankind**. *Nature*, 415 (6867): 23. ——译者注

version, called "différance", with an "a".

这种宇宙学的思辨性和**述行性**（performative），将导致一种从人类纪（Anthropocene）通向我拟命名为逆人类纪（Neganthropocene）的理论和实践的前景与计划——所有这些问题都将被置于**热力学的宇宙学效应这一语境**中进行讨论，它包括作为热力学第二定律的熵的观念，以及**在负熵性的颠倒和分叉（negentropic inversions and bifurcations）意上对生命和技术的分析**，不过这种颠倒和分叉**不是反对熵**，而是在类似于德里达在《哲学的边缘》(*Marges de la Philosophie*) 中所说的带"a"的"延异（différance）"①过程中，通过延缓熵而使熵发生转移。

This diversion is, **in the case of technics** (that is, **organology**), a **pharmacology**, and it constitutes **a *future*, an *avenir***, within the irreversible law of entropic becoming,

ENTROPIC BECOMING/ NEGENTROPIC FUTURE

devenir—a **becoming** that, insofar as it is **inherently entropic**,

---

① "延异（différance）"是德里达独创的一个术语，它用法文词"差异（différence）"的发音相同，只是用字母"a"取代了字母"e"，旨在通过这个差异性的"a"来解构西方语言和思想制度（包括西方的语言和哲学传统）的直接同一性。该术语是理解德里达解构主义哲学的一个核心范畴。——译者注

then **becomes the law of what had hitherto and without major objection been referred to as "being"**, that is, until 1924, the year of the discovery by **Edwin Hubble** of the **expansion of the universe**, opening the era of what Ilya Prigogine calls the **evolutionary perspective in physics.**

在技术（即**器官学**）的意义上，这种转移就是一种**药理学**（pharmacology），它将在不可逆的熵的生成（becoming, *devenir*）规律中建构*一种未来*（*future*, *avenir*）——这种生成具有内在的熵性，已经成为迄今为止普遍接受的"存在"规律：直到 1924 年，**埃德温·哈勃**（**Edwin Hubble**）① 发现了**宇宙膨胀**（**expansion of the universe**），从而打开了伊利亚·普里高津（Ilya Prigogine）② 所说的**物理学上的进化论**时代。

---

① 埃德温·哈勃（Edwin Hubble, 1889—1953）：美国天文学家，先后在芝加哥大学天文台、威尔逊天文台工作，1923—1924 年发现造父变星，1929 年发现哈勃定律，为宇宙膨胀说开辟道路。其代表作有：《星云世界》（1936）、《宇宙观测法》（1937）等。——译者注

② 伊利亚·普里高津（Ilya Prigogine, 1917—2003）：比利时化学家、物理学家，非平衡态统计物理与耗散结构理论奠基人，曾获得诺贝尔化学奖（1977）。其代表作有：《结构、耗散和生命》（1969）等。——译者注

SIXTH COURSE
9 APRIL 2016
/
Thermodynamics, Gestell
and Neganthropology

第 六 讲

2016.4.9

热力学、座架和负人类学

2. Generality, Metaphysics, Cosmology
一般性，形而上学，宇宙学

What does the adjective "**general**" mean in the expressions *general ecology* used by Erich Hörl and *general organology* as I try to think it? Is it the same as what Georges Bataille was referring to in his thought of **general economy in this book**?①

Does this "generality" inevitably lead us back to a *metaphysica generalis*—or to a *metaphysica speculativa*? THAT IS, TO IDEALISM?

---

① The question of the generality of Bataille's general economy, which will be explored in depth in *La Société automatique 2. L'avenir du savoir* (forthcoming), has been introduced in *La Société automatique 1. L'avenir du travail* in order to counter the point of view developed by Claude Lévi-Strauss at the end of *Tristes Tropiques*, where he likens anthropology to an "entropology", which I oppose by passing through Bataille and in terms of the question of a neganthropology that would also be an organology and a pharmacology.

在埃里希·霍尔（Erich Hörl）所说的"一般生态学"和我在思考的"一般器官学"中的这个形容词"**一般的**"是什么意思呢？它与乔治·巴塔耶在《被诅咒的部分》(*La Part maudite*) **这本书**中的**一般经济学**思想一样吗？①这种"一般性（generality）"必然会将我们带回到一种*一般形而上学*(*metaphysica generalis*)，还是回到一种*思辨形而上学*(*metaphysica speculativa*)呢？即回到唯心主义（IDEALISM）呢？

These questions must be explored in **dialogue with Whitehead and Simondon**, that is, with, respectively, ***concrescence* as that process which is the subject of Whitehead's *Process and Reality*, and the *process of concretization*②**, which is one of the main concepts of Simondon's *Du mode d'existence des objets techniques*—by **raising the question of**

---

① 对于巴塔耶的一般经济学中的一般性问题，我已经在《自动社会1. 工作的未来》(*La Société automatique 1. L'avenir du travail*) 中做了介绍，并将会在《自动社会2. 知识的未来》(*La Société automatique 2. L'avenir du savoir*)（即将出版）中做深入阐述，以解释列维-施特劳斯在《忧郁的热带》(*Tristes Tropiques*) 中把人类学比作一种"熵学"的观点。从一种负人类学问题亦即一种器官学和药理学问题的角度来说，我反对忽视巴塔耶。

② But also with the concept of grammatization, that is, discretization, which is also to say, with respect to the question of categorization as *condition of concretization*—this reference to categorization pointing here towards a hypothesis formulated by IRI in relation to the web: we posit that the web must see its general architecture evolving in the direction of the constitution of a hermeneutic web, itself founded on a graphic language of contributory annotation, a platform for sharing notes and a hermeneutic social network.

the generality of the point of view of *process*, and as **passage from abstraction to concretion, or to concrescence,** *the abstract and the concrete* being conceived here, therefore, from **a fundamentally and primordially processual point of view.**

这些问题必须**在与怀特海**①**和西蒙栋的对话中**加以探讨，即分别**结合**怀特海在《过程与实在》（*Process and Reality*）之**主题的过程**和作为西蒙栋《技术客体的存在方式》（*Du mode d'existence des objets techniques*）的主要概念之一的**具体化过程**②（*the process of concretization*）来加以理解——**通过提出从抽象到具体或从抽象到结合（concrescence）的意义上的过程观点的一般性问题**来加以探究。因此，这里需要从一种根本性的、原真性的过程视角来加以思考。

We will have a presentation by Wu dedicated to Simondon on next Wednesday, and we will discuss this

---

① 阿尔弗雷德·诺思·怀特海（Alfred North Whitehead, 1861—1947）：英国数学家、哲学家、教育理论家，过程哲学创始人。其代表作有：《数学原理》（1910—1913）、《过程与实在》（1929）等。——译者注

② 但这也涉及编程化（grammatization）概念或离散化（discretization）概念，也就是说，涉及作为**具体化**(concretization) 之条件的范畴化（categorization）问题——这里所说的范畴化是指由一种与网络相关的 IRI 所制定的假说：我们假设这种网络必须看到它在一种解释学网络结构趋向中的一般体系结构进化，它自身就建立在一种有助于注解的图形语言、一种为了分享注释的平台和一种解释性社会网络之上。

furthermore.

下周三吴同学①将会做一个关于西蒙栋的报告，我们到时候会深入讨论这一点。

In addition, these questions lead us back to that *cosmology* which passes through Simondon and Whitehead—**beyond the rational cosmology of Kant**, who **could not**, precisely, **take into account the** *organological* **question**（any more than could philosophy in general, with the **exception of Marx**）.

此外，这些问题会将我们带回到贯穿西蒙栋和怀特海的**宇宙学**——它**超越了康德的理性宇宙学**，康德还没有准确**思考器官学问题**（他至多是在思考哲学一般问题，而**马克思是个例外**）。

The ideas of a rational cosmology are in Kant those of **reason** (see *The Transcendental Dialectic*, chapter 2, "The Antinomy of Pure Reason"), and we shall see that **Whitehead sees himself in some respects from a similar**

---

① 吴宁宁，河海大学马克思主义学院的博士后人员，科技哲学博士，研究方向是技术哲学，报告的拟定题目是《个体化的三个层次》，内容为西蒙栋的《论个人发生问题》(*The Position Of The Problem Of Ontogenesis*) 一文与梅洛-庞蒂的《行为的结构》的对比性研究。——译者注

perspective. Nevertheless, it is **impossible to think** with this apparatus alone the **thermodynamic question** such as it was constituted with Sadi Carnot as the *theory of the steam engine*.

在康德那里，理性宇宙学思想是属于**理性**观念（参见《先验辩证法》[*The Transcendental Dialectic*] 第二章《纯粹理性的二律背反》["The Antinomy of Pure Reason"]）。我们可以看到，怀海特认为自己在某些方面采取了相似的视角。不管怎样，只借助这种工具（apparatus）来思考**热力学问题**（thermodynamic question）是不可能的，比如萨迪·卡诺（Sadi Carnot）就曾把热力学问题建构为***蒸汽机理论***（*theory of the steam engine*）。

Kantianism, in fact, is constituted by a **denial of the organological conditions** of the formation of **reason** as well as of **understanding**. This **does not allow for any thought of entropy** such as **Carnot** understands it **on the basis of the artefact** that is the **steam engine as closed thermodynamic system**. Nor does it allow for consideration, therefore, of those regimes of **negative entropy** or **"low entropy"** that were uncovered by **Erwin Schrödinger**, preceded by **Henri Bergson**[①], then by

---

[①] As Nicholas Georgescu-Roegen recalls.

Claude Shannon, Léon Brillouin and Nicholas Georgescu-Roegen, who, unlike his predecessors, insisted on the issue of exosomatic organs.

实际上，康德主义是通过**否定理性**和**知性**形成的**器官学条件**而建立的，因此**不会产生任何关于熵的思想**，比如**卡诺（Carnot）**就是**基于人造物（artefact）**即蒸汽机而将其理解为**封闭的热力系统**。因而康德主义也不会考虑**负熵（negative entropy）（低熵［low entropy］）**状态。这是由埃尔温·薛定谔（Erwin Schrödinger）发现，**亨利·柏格森（Henri Bergson）**①②推进，然后由**克劳德·香农（Claude Shannon）**③、**莱昂·布里渊（Léon Brillouin）**④和**尼古拉斯·乔治斯库-罗根（Nicholas Georgescu-Roegen）**进一步发展的理论。但与前人不同的是，乔治斯库-罗根坚持关注体外器官（exo-somatic organs）问题。

---

① 正如尼古拉斯·乔治斯库-罗根所回忆的那样。
② 亨利·柏格森（Henri Bergson，1859—1941）：法国哲学家，诺贝尔文学奖获得者（1927）。曾任职于巴黎高等师范学院、法兰西学院，当选法兰西科学院院士（1914）。其代表作有：《物质与记忆》（1896）、《创造进化论》（1907）等。——译者注
③ 克劳德·艾尔伍德·香农（Claude Elwood Shannon，1916—2001）：美国数学家、电子工程师和密码学家，被誉为信息论的创始人。其代表作有：《通信的数学理论》（1948/1949）等。——译者注
④ 莱昂·尼古拉·布里渊（Léon Nicolas Brillouin，1889—1969）：法国物理学家、数学家，美国国家科学院院士（1953）。提出布里渊区、布里渊散射等理论。其代表作有：《超高频无线电数学》（1943）等。——译者注

I have tried to show, in *Technics and Time, 3*, why the **Kantian schematism**, fruit of the **transcendental imagination, did not allow him to think the organological** (that is, **tertiary retention**) and its consequences for any idea of reason (including the idea of rational cosmology).① From the organological perspective I defend here, **the schematism originally comes from technical exteriorisation and the artefactualization of the world** as the condition of the **constitution** of the world, that is, as condition of the **projection in the world of concepts** *constituting* **the given data of intuition** of this world such as **it is** *ordered* **in the** *cosmos*—and it is **the consideration of the cosmos itself** (and not just of the world) that hence **finds itself affected**—we access the cosmos **as cosmos** on the basis of **hypomnesic tertiary retentions** in all their forms, **from the shaman's instruments to Herschel's telescope.**

在《技术与时间·3》(*Technics and Time, 3*) 中，我试图阐明康德的作为先验想象之结果的图式论 (**schematism**) 为什么会阻碍他从器官学（即第三持存）及

---

① For in fact, if what reason produces is not concepts but rather ideas, that extend the pure concepts of understanding beyond their regime of legality, which is experience given by intuition, and if these concepts are themselves conditioned by schemas conditioned by hypomnesic tertiary retention, as I argue in *Technics and Time, 3*, then the ideas of reason are themselves also conditioned by tertiary retention.

其结果角度来思考任何理性观念（包括理性宇宙论观念）①的原因。从器官学角度，我认为，**图式论源自于世界的技术外化**（technical exteriorisation）**和人造物化**（artefactualization），它们是这个世界的**构成条件**，也是**概念世界的投射条件。概念世界构成**了这个世界的既定的直观数据，比如它**在宇宙中是*组织有序的*——**而且，它是对宇宙本身（不只是这个世界）以及宇宙由此**发现自身也受到影响**的思考：我们基于**超级记忆第三持存**（hypomnesic tertiary retentions）的各种形式即从巫师的仪器到赫谢尔（Herschel）的望远镜来接近作为宇宙的宇宙。

Since the time of **ancient philosophy**, the *kosmos*, **as an arrangement** [*disposition*] of *physis*, through which it lets itself be seen and thus *appear* (phenomenalize itself) as this very arrangement, and **as an** *order*②, this *kosmos* has been **conceived in terms of spheres and cycles closed in upon themselves as a <u>fundamental and absolute equilibrium</u>.**

---

① 实际上，如果理性产生的不是概念，而是观念，那么，纯粹知性概念就超出了它们的合法性范围即直觉赋予的经验。如果这些知性概念本身是以受超级记忆第三持存制约的图式为条件的，正如我在《技术与时间·3》中指出的那样，那么，理性观念本身也是受第三持存所制约的。

② This order is that of the "parure" that is the kosmos as *that which appears*, according to a translation by Beaufret (*Dialogue avec Heidegger 1*).

自古典哲学时代以来，作为一种*自然*（*physis*）**安排**的**宇宙**（*kosmos*），借助自然来展现自身，（通过使自身现象化）而呈现为这种自然安排和**一种*规则*（*order*）**①。**宇宙在天体范围和周期循环上已经被认为自身具有一种根本的、绝对的平衡（fundamental and absolute equilibrium）。**

In Aristotle's *Metaphysics*, which localizes the **sublunary world** in the **fixed sphere, technics, which constitutes the organological condition, is in relation to the sublunary as the region of contingency** and of **"what can be otherwise than it is"** (*to endekhomenon allos ekhein*), whereas the *eide*, **conceived in relation to cosmic fixities, opposes to this facticity the necessity of** *to on*. This division will be maintained in Kant, and this is particularly clear in *Theory and Practice*.

在亚里士多德的《形而上学》中，他将**地上世界**

---

① 根据波伏勒（Beaufret）在《与海德格尔对话·1》（*Dialogue avec Heidegger 1*）中的一种翻译，这种规则就是宇宙所显现出来的"珍宝（parure, jewel）"规则。(根据《与海德格尔对话·1》英文版，赫拉克利特、荷马等古典思想家以珍宝的特性来比喻宇宙的规则，即珍宝不仅能够自我发光，而且能够规定［valorize］其穿戴者。与其说珠宝是为自身发光，不如说它是为他者闪耀。宇宙具有与珍宝相似的性质。) 参见 Jean Beaufret (2006) *Dialogue With Heidegger: Greek Philosophy*, trans. Mark Sinclair, Bloomington and Indianapolis. Indiana University Press, p. 7. 以及 Jean Beaufret (1973) *Dialogue avec Heidegger: Philosophie Grecque*. Paris: Les Éditions De Minuit, p. 25.——译者注

(sublunary world) 定位在固定领域, 而构成器官学条件的技术是与作为偶然性和 "必然性（what can be otherwise than it is, [*to endekhomenon allos ekhein*]）" 领域的地上世界相关的, 然而, 与宇宙固定性 (cosmic fixities) 有关的*理念*(*eide*)① 则是与*存在*(*to on*) 的必要性和真实性相对立的。这种分离在康德那里被保留下来, 尤其是在《理论与实践》(*Theory and Practice*) 中清楚可见。

And we can see how Engels, even if he introduces a dynamic in the universe, cannot understand how and why the stake on entropy is the expansion of the universe as its cooling.

Temperature of space even by a millionth of a degree centigrade. What becomes of all this enormous quantity of heat? Is it for ever dissipated in the attempt to heat universal space, has it ceased to exist practically, and does it only continue to exist

---

① "eide" 是希腊文 eidos 的复数形式, eidos (εἶδος) 与 idea (ἰδέα) 为同义词, 在词源学上, eidos 出自动词 "eidein"（看）, 与 "εἴδομαι"（显现、看似、显似）和 "ἰδεῖν/εἶδον"（看）有着共同的词根, 意指 "被看到的东西"、"所见之物的外表和形态"。自柏拉图以来, 它被确立为一个重要的哲学概念, 意指事物的形式、类型、共相或本质, 是一种与具体事物相对立的、超感性的抽象实在。在中国学界, 对于此概念的翻译和阐释一直存在争论, 此处使用的是它的通常译法。——译者注

theoretically, in the fact that universal space has become warmer by a decimal fraction of a degree beginning with ten or more noughts? The indestructibility of motion forbids such an assumption, but it allows the possibility that by the successive falling into one another of the bodies of the universe all existing mechanical motion will be converted into heat and the latter radiated into space, so that in spite of all "indestructibility of force" all motion in general would have ceased. (Incidentally it is seen here how inaccurate is the term "indestructibility of force" instead of "indestructibility of motion".) Hence we arrive at the conclusion that in some way, which it will later be the task of scientific research to demonstrate, the heat radiated into space must be able to become transformed into another form of motion, in which it can once more be stored up and rendered active. Thereby the chief difficulty in the way of the reconversion of extinct suns into incandescent vapour disappears.

For the rest, the eternally repeated succession of worlds in infinite time is only the logical complement to the co-existence of innumerable worlds in infinite space—a principle the necessity of which has forced itself even on the anti-theoretical Yankee brain of Draper.

我们可以看到，恩格斯——尽管他介绍了宇宙动力学——无法理解熵是如何和为什么是宇宙随着自身的冷却而发生扩张的结果：

这全部的巨大热量变成了什么呢？它是不是永远用于为宇宙空间供暖的尝试，是不是实际上已不复存在而只在理论上仍然存在于宇宙空间的温度已上升百亿分之一度或更低度数这一事实中？这个假定否认了运动的不灭性，它认可这样一种可能由于诸天体不断地相互碰在一起，一切现存的机械运动都变为热，而且这种热将发散到宇宙空间中去，因此尽管存在"力的不灭性"，一切运动还是会停下来（在这里顺便可以看出，用力的不灭性这个说法替代运动的不灭性这个说法，是多么错误）。于是我们得出这样一个结论：发散到宇宙空间中去的热一定有可能通过某种途径（指明这一途径，将是以后某个时候自然研究的课题）转变为另一种运动形式，在这种运动形式中，它能够重新集结和活动起来。因此，阻碍已死的太阳重新转化为炽热气团的主要困难便消除了。

此外，诸天体在无限时间内永恒重复的先后相继，不过是无数天体在无限空间内同时并存的逻辑补充——这一原理的必然性，甚至德雷帕的反理论的美国人头脑也不得不承认了。①

---

① 《马克思恩格斯文集》第 9 卷，人民出版社，2009 年版，第 425—426 页。——译者注

3. Combustion
燃烧

The advent of the **thermodynamic *machine***, which Heidegger does not take into account, nevertheless constitutes, with the **automation** of machines, **what Heidegger refers to as the *Ereignis* of "modern technics"** (that is, of the industrial revolution) and **its *Gestell*** — and this is also **the advent ("*Ereignis*")** of what today we refer to as the Anthropocene, <u>but not as an Er-Eignis, that is, a co-propriation, as the French translators of Heidegger wrongly claimed, but rather as an expropriation,</u> wherein <u>the human world appears to constitute a *fundamental disruption* of the cosmos, and of its local (planetary) equilibriums.</u>

不管怎样，**热力机**的出现，这是海德格尔没有考虑到的，伴随着机器的**自动化**，构成了**海德格尔所指的"现代技术"**（即工业革命）**的**生成（*Ereignis*）及其*座架*

(***Gestell***)——这也是我们今天所说的人类纪的到来（即"*生成*[*Ereignis*]"）。**但是人类纪不是一种生-成（Er-Eignis）即一种共同-占有（co-proporiation），正如海德格尔著作的法译者错误主张的那样，而是一种外在-占有（ex-propriation），在这里人类世界似乎构成了宇宙及其地方性（行星的）平衡的根本中断。**

The **thermodynamic** *machine* is, however, *also* what **introduces the question of an irreducible processuality of the cosmos itself**, of the **irreversibility of** becoming, and, if not the instability, then at least **the processuality in which this becoming consists**, and it introduces all this **at the heart of physics itself.** This question seems, however, to have **remained hidden in Heidegger due to his fixation on cybernetics** (which seems equally to mask the question of **marketing**—in Heidegger as well as in Hans Jonas—such as Deleuze attempted to think it *Modern Thermodynamics*: *From Heat Engines to Dissipative Structures* as that **knowledge characteristic of societies of control**).①

然而，热力机也**带来了宇宙本身的不可还原的过程性**

---

① Gilles Deleuze (1995) *Negotiations*: *1972-1990*. trans. Martin Joughin. New York: Columbia University Press.

（irreducible processuality of the cosmos itself）和生成的不可逆性（the irreversibility of becoming）问题。而这种生成如果没有不稳定性，至少也具有过程性，这构成了物理学的核心问题。然而，这个问题似乎仍然隐含在海德格尔的思想中，因为他执着于控制论（cybernetics）（这似乎同样遮蔽了**市场营销**［marketing］问题——在海德格尔和汉斯·尤纳斯［Hans Jonas］那里都是如此——譬如，德勒兹就试图将市场营销［《现代热力学：从热机到耗散结构》］看作控制社会的知识特性）。①

The thermodynamic machine—which in *physics* raises the specific and new problem of the dissipation of energy and, more generally, of the irreversibility of the **"arrow of time"** oriented towards **disorder**, that is, the **irreversible increase of entropy**—is also **an industrial technical object** that, arranged with the first automatisms and establishing *__proletarianization__* (that is, loss of knowledge) as the *fundamental principle of productivity*, fundamentally **disrupts** *social* **organizations,** and at the same time **radically alters "the understanding that Dasein has of its being".**

---

① 中译本参见［法］吉尔·德勒兹：《哲学与权力的谈判——德勒兹访谈录》，刘汉全译，商务印书馆，2000 年版。——译者注

热力机在*物理学*中引出了一个特殊的新问题，即能量的耗散问题。更一般地说，就是导向**无序**即**不可逆的熵的增加**的"时间箭头（arrow of time）"的不可逆性问题。热力机也是**一种工业技术客体**，它受第一次自动主义的安排，将**无产阶级化**（即知识的丧失）确立为*生产力的基本原则*（*fundamental principle of productivity*），从根本上**打破了社会组织**，同时**彻底改变了**"此在对其存在的理解（the understanding that Dasein has of its being）"。

If proletarianization radically disrupts social organization, the **thermodynamic machine also transforms the scientific point of view.** Consisting essentially in a *combustion*, this technical object—an element of which, the **flyball governor**, will prove critical for conceiving **cybernetics**—introduced, on both the **physical plane** and the **ecological plane**, *the question of human fire and of its pharmacology*, which is thereby inscribed **at the heart of the thought of the cosmos** *as cosmos* (both from the perspective of physics and from that of anthropological ecology), the play between them being **both cosmic and mundane**: this is what the **Promethean myth of fire** means in Greek tragedy.

如果无产阶级化彻底打破了社会组织，**热力机也会改**

变科学的观点。这种技术客体的本质在于**燃烧**——它的一个零件即**飞球调速器**（flyball governor）将证明它对于**控制论构想是关键性的**——它在**物理领域**和**生态领域**都提出了**人造火及其药理学的问题**（*question of human fire and of its pharmacology*），并因此被标定为**作为宇宙的宇宙思想**（the thought of the cosmos as cosmos）**的中心**（从物理学角度和人类学-生态学角度来看）。它们之间的作用既是**宇宙性的**（cosmic），也是**世俗性的**（mundane）：这就是希腊悲剧中**普罗米修斯盗火之谜**。

The notion of the ***Anthropocene*** can **appear** as such only from the moment **when the question of the cosmos reveals itself to be that of combustion**, accomplishing the **transformation of cosmology into an astrophysics of combustion**, and as **emerging from the thermodynamic question opened and posed by the steam engine—by the techno-logical conquest of fire**. Only **within this perspective** can there occur the **kenosis (from Hegel) of the "death of God"**.

人类纪的观念只有在这种契机下才会**出现**，即当宇宙问题被揭示为燃烧问题，从而完成从宇宙学向燃烧的天体物理学的转变，并开始出现由蒸汽机——**火的技术-逻辑征服**（the techno-logical conquest of fire）——所打开和提出的热力学问题。只有在这个意义上，这种"上帝已死"意义上的（来自黑格尔的）对神性的放弃（kenosis）才会发生。

As a problem of physics, **the techno-logical conquest of fire (which is the *Ereignis* of *Gestell* on the basis of which proletarianization arises as *Bestand*)** placed *anthropogenesis at the heart of concrescence*, that is, <u>organological organogenesis</u> (what Georgescu-Roegen therefore calls the **exosomatic**), and as the <u>*local technicization of the cosmos*</u>—local and **therefore** *relative*. But **this leads to a** *complete rethinking* **of the cosmos from an astrophysical perspective,** *starting from this position and* <u>**from this local opening of the question of fire**</u>, and **as a** *pharmakon* **of which we must** *take care*, that is the role, in greek mythology, of the goddess Hestia which we must tend, and **such that the question of the** *energy* **it harbours constitutes the** *matrix of the thought of life as the play of entropy and negentropy*. ①

---

① I have elsewhere argued, in... and in *La Société automatique 1. L'avenir du travail* that these conceptual mutations of physics and of cosmology-become-astrophysics also involve a mutation of the notion of work, which becomes force measured in watts (force being what Aristotelian metaphysics conceived as *dunamis*), and no longer conceived as *energeia*, that is, as *noetic act*, that is, as *individuation*. It is this transformation that also makes possible that proletarianization that occurs when the steam engine combines with the automatisms made possible by the mechanical tertiary retention characteristic of industrial mechanization.

作为一个物理学问题，火的技术-逻辑征服（它是*座架的生成*[the *Ereignis of Gestell*]，无产阶级化在此基础上成为一种*持存*[*Bestand*]）将人类起源（*anthropogenesis*）置于共生（*concrescence*）的核心地位，这种共生就是*器官学意义上的器官形成*（*organological organogenesis*）（因此乔治斯库-罗根称之为外在化［the **exosomatic**］）和*宇宙的地方性技术化*（*local technicization of the cosmos*）——因为是地方性的，**因此是**相对的。但是，**这会引导我们从天体物理学的角度来彻底重新思考宇宙。也就是从这样一种立场出发，从关于火的问题的地方性开端出发，我们必须将火看作一种药**，这是希腊神话中灶神赫斯提亚（Hestia）[①] 的工作，**这样，它所包含的*能量*问题就将信息和生命思想的基体建构为*熵和负熵的作用***。[②]

The **cosmos** certainly becomes the **universe** well before this, with **Nicholas of Cusa** and **Giordano Bruno**——this is his

---

[①] 赫斯提亚（希腊语：Εστα，译为"炉"或"炉边"）：希腊神话中的灶神，又称火焰女神，掌万民的家庭事务。十二神之一，在诸神中具有崇高的地位。火焰象征着家庭和生命的存在与延续。——译者注

[②] 我在其他地方如《自动社会·1：工作的未来》（*La Société automatique 1. L'avenir du travail*）中说过，物理学上的观念变异和宇宙学-天体物理学（cosmology-become-astrophysics）上的观念变异也是一种工作观念的变异，即变为以多少瓦特来衡量的力（force）（这种力就是亚里士多德的形而上学所认为的爆炸力[*dunamis*]），而不再被看作是活动（*energeia*），即智力活动（*noetic act*），即个体化（*individuation*）。正是这种转变也使无产阶级化成为可能，即当蒸汽机与因工业机械化的机械第三持存特性而成为可能的自动主义联合时，无产阶级化就发生了。

statue, in Roma, on the place where he perished in fire. But **it is only with thermodynamics that the cosmos becomes not only the infinite universe, but the astrophysical "consumption" of becoming.**

在此之前，在**库萨的尼古拉**（Nicholas of Cusa）和**乔尔丹诺·布鲁诺**（Giordano Bruno）——上页图是他在罗马被火烧死的地方建起的雕像①——那里，**宇宙**（cosmos）确实变成了**世界**（universe）。然而，**只是随着热力学的产生，宇宙才变成天体物理学意义上的生成的"消耗"**。

The discovery of the notion of **entropy natively presupposes the *experience* of *anthropic fire*,** so to speak, as the entropy of **physical combustion**, then as the negentropy of **vital combustion**, if we can put it this way, **through which the living finds its place, its locality and its** *ethos* **in the universe that is carried along in the dissipative movement of its disorder,** and **where the living, insofar as it is not immortal, nor therefore divine,** *always returns* **to cosmic entropy**—including as the **production of methane by animals**, which can lead

---

① 乔尔丹诺·布鲁诺（Giordano Bruno, 1548—1600）：意大利思想家、自然科学家、哲学家和文学家。因捍卫和发展哥白尼的日心说，反对教会的地心说，于1592年被捕入狱，1600年2月17日被宗教裁判所判为"异端"而烧死在罗马鲜花广场。其代表作有：《论无限、宇宙和众世界》（1584）等。——译者注

to the biospherical disequilibrium of the ozone layer and so on, that is, well before their return to inertia.

> Genesis 3:19 New international
> Version (NIV)
> "By the sweat of your brow
> you will eat your food
> until you return to the ground,
> since from it you were taken;
> for dust you are
> and to dust you will return."

熵的观念的发现**本来是以人造火**(*anthropic fire*)的经验为前提的,也就是说,作为**物理燃烧**的熵,然后是作为**生命燃烧**的负熵,如果沿着这个思路,那么生命就在世界(**universe**)中找到了它的场域(**place**)、位置(**locality**)和气质(*ethos*)。这个宇宙伴有自身无序的耗散运动,<u>在这个宇宙中,生命不是永生的,因而不是神,而是总是回到宇宙性的熵</u>——包括动物产生的甲烷,它们在恢复惰性状况之前,会导致生物圈的臭氧层失衡。

4. *Organology of the question*
器官学问题

It is doubtful whether the full dimension of the **question of entropy and negentropy among human beings, as a *question*** , has ever truly been grasped.① We could show, for example, that **the works dedicated to entropy by Henri Atlan and Edgar Morin take no account whatsoever of the specificity of organological (exosomatic) negentropy,** nor obviously of the equally **specific entropy that it generates**—in particular since the advent of the Anthropocene. And we could also show that **the theory of information conceived as regime of entropy and negentropy is itself thereby fundamentally weakened (Simondon included).**②

人类中的熵和负熵问题的全面内涵是否被理解是令人

---

① In the sense that I attempted to redefine this as a question, as *creating* a question, in *What Makes Life Worth Living*.

② On this subject, see my *Qu'appelle-t-on penser?*, forthcoming, developed further in *La Société automatique 2*.

怀疑的。它<u>作为一个问题</u>，还尚未被真正把握。① 我们可以看到，比如，专门研究熵的亨利·阿特兰（Henri Atlan）和埃德加·莫兰（Edgar Morin）没有考虑器官学意义上的（外在化的）负熵的特殊性，也明显没有考虑它引起的具体的熵——尤其是自人类纪到来之后。我们也会看到，被认为是属于熵和负熵领域的信息理论本身也发生了根本性的衰落（西蒙栋也包括在列）。②

At the beginning of the nineteenth century, **technics establishes, scientifically but also socially (as standardization and proletarianization), the** *question* **of entropy and negentropy as** *the* **crucial** *problem* **of the everyday life of human beings and of life in general**, and, ultimately, of the universe as a whole, which once again becomes the *kosmos* insofar as it invites, hosts and in some way houses the negentropic, that is, the living, including *noetic* **life, which we therefore ought to call the** *neganthropo-logical*.

NEGANTHROPO-LOGICAL

19世纪初，技术（technics）在科学意义上和（作为标

---

① 在这个意义上，我在《什么让生命值得活》（*What Makes Life Worth Living*）中试图重新将它定义为一个问题，就像开创一个问题。
② 关于这个主题，参见我即将出版的《何谓思？》（*Qu'appelle-t-on penser?*），并在《自动社会·2》中做了进一步发展。

准化和无产阶级化的）社会意义上带来了熵和负熵的*问题*，这些问题成为人们的日常生活、一般生命乃至整个宇宙的关键*难题*。这样，整个宇宙就再次变为吸引（invite）、主宰（host）和以某种方式安置（house）负熵即包括<u>*智性生命*（*noetic life*）</u>在内的生活方式（living）的宇宙。<u>所以，我们应该将这种智性生命称为负人类学-逻辑</u>（the negan-thropo-logical）。

As such, that is, **as the organogenesis of this *anthropos* that is not self-sufficient, technics**—which is also anthropic

ANTHROPIC

in the sense that it extends and accelerates the entropy

THE ENTROPY OF ANTHROPIZATION IN THE ANTHROPOCENE

of anthropization in the Anthropocene—**constitutes the matrix of all thought of the *oikos*, of habitat and of its law as *ecology* as well as *economy***, which is also to say, as *oikonomia* (which can here be "general" only in George Bataille's a-theological sense).

这样一来，技术作为不能自足的人类器官发生，它——从技术在人类纪中使人类化的熵（the entropy of anthropization）发生扩展和加速的意义上来说，技术也是属人的（anthropic）——构成了一切生态学（*oikos*）思想、栖居地（**habitat**）思想和作为*生态学*与*经济学*即家政学（*oikonomia*）（这里的"一般的"只是在乔治·巴塔耶的非神学[a-theological]意义上而言的）规律的基体（**matrix**）。

This is also what was going on with what was hitherto conceived as **hermeneutic knowledge of the mind**. This eventually became, with the **utilization by cognitivism of the concept of information**—as it will be **thought by information theory and computationalist cybernetics**—a new "**science of the mind**" (as well as *spirit*, *Geist*), in which **mind and spirit find themselves folded back into "cognition"**.

这也就是我们将利用迄今所说的**思想的诠释性知识**（**hermeneutic knowledge of the mind**）来继续展开的东西。由于**信息概念对它（技术）的认知主义使用**——这也将是**信息理论和计算主义控制论的考察对象**——它将最终变成一种新的"思想科学"（和精神科学），由此思想和精神都将归于"认知"。

In this **new metaphysics that is cognitivism**, the organological question that *makes possible* such a perspective (where the **computer** assumed to be a **"Turing machine"** as it is also the fiction of the movie *The Imitation Game*, but many people today contest this use and interpretation of Turing, and particularly Jean Lassègue as well as David Bates becomes the **model of the mind**) is **never posed**. You can find developments on that in the book *Digital Studies* with a chapter written by Bates.

在这种新的认知主义的形而上学中,器官学问题使这样一种观点成为可能(即计算机被假定为一种"图灵机器[Turing machine]",虽然它也是《模仿游戏》(*The Imitation Game*)这部电影的虚构,但今天很多人都在争论关于图灵的使用和解释,尤其是让·拉塞格(Jean Lassègue)和大卫·贝特斯(David Bates)的观点已成为这种思想的典型),但器官学问题本身却从来没有被提出。你们可以在我的《数字化研究》(*Digital Studies*)中贝特斯(Bates)写的一章中看到关于这一点的推进。

"Organological" means here, **that which causes the living to pass from the organic stage to the organological stage**, which requires radically **new terms with which to think the organization of that of which this new organogenesis is the condition.**

这里,"器官学的"意味着:它促使生命从器官阶段(organic stage)进入器官学阶段(organological stage),这在根本上需要用全新的术语来思考以新的器官发生为条件的组织。

Technics—as the advent and event of what **Ernst Kapp** and then **Friedrich Engels** called **"projection" or "organic extension"**, but which more precisely is **an *organological* extension**, an extension **that is *not* organic** —is the pursuit of life by means other than life.

技术——正如**恩斯特·卡普**①和**弗里德里希·恩格斯**曾称之为"**投射**"或"**器官延伸(organic extension)**",但更准确地说,它是**一种*器官学延伸*(*organological* extension)**,而**不是一种器官延伸**——是生命借助生命之外的手段而追求的东西。

And this is also **the opening of what Heidegger believed should still be called the "question of being" as the advent of *Dasein*, that is, of the "being who questions".**

---

① 恩斯特·卡普(Ernst Kapp, 1808—1896):德国技术哲学家、政治活动家,技术哲学奠基者。其代表作有:《比较地理学》(1845)、《技术哲学纲要》(1877)等。——译者注

这也是**海德格尔**认为仍应该将"**存在的问题**（question of being）"看作*此在出现*（the advent of *Dasein*）即"**追问的存在**（being who questions）"出现的开端。

Contrary to this Heideggerian perspective, we posit that **if *Dasein* questions, it can only be insofar as *technics challenges it*, *puts it into question***—and does so starting from the fact that **it is required to *formulate* this challenge, that is, to exteriorize it, which is very often** (if it is indeed a question and not a fantasy or chatter) **the starting point for a new technical exteriorisation** and **a new putting in question, a new challenge, and so on.** Such a vicious circle is the stake of Freud's discontent in culture.

与海德格尔的观点不同，我们认为，**如果*此在*追问了，那也只能是*技术挑战了此在*，使它成为问题**——之所以这样是因为这样的事实，即**它需要规定这种挑战，使它外化，而且通常是**（如果它真是一个问题，而不是一种幻想或唠叨）**一种新的技术外化、一个新问题和一种新挑战等的出发点**。这种恶性循环就是弗洛伊德在《文明与缺憾》（*Civilization and Discontents*）一书中所说的文化缺憾的主要方面（stake）。

As this **organogenesis** that is **at once anthropic and neganthropic,**

ANTHROPIC AND
NEGANTHROPIC

technics is the *post-Darwinian* evolution of life that has
become *essentially technical and organological*, **and not just
organic.** This technical form of life poses in **completely new
terms** the problem of **what Canguilhem called the infidelity of
the milieu,** which confronts living things in general each time
their milieu changes, but **which, in the case of** *technical* **life,
constitutes a** *technical milieu* **that introduces a new type of infidelity,** in which **it is organological and not just organic life
that ceaselessly disrupts its milieu,** and does so **structurally** and
ever more rapidly: structurally to the extent that **this
disruption is vital to it,** but **tragically** to the extent that **it is
always also toxic** —insofar as **it constitutes a phase difference
that cannot be transindividuated, that is, adopted,** in the
sense that it must be individuated both psychically and
socially (this is what **Niklas Luhmann,** it seems to me, does
not see).

由于这种器官形成既是属人的（anthropic），又是负人

南京课程：在人类纪时代阅读马克思和恩格斯
186

的（neganthropic），技术是*后达尔文式的生命进化*（*post-Darwinian evolution of life*），因此生命进化在本质上已变成*技术的和器官学的*，而不是器官的。生命的这种技术形式提出了一个全新的术语问题，即康吉莱姆所说的环境的背叛（the infidelity of the milieu）。一般生命体在每次环境发生变化时就要面对这种情况。但在*由技术生命构成的技术环境中产生了一种新型的背叛，即在技术环境中，这种器官学的、不只是器官的生命不断地破坏它的环境，并结构性地乃至更快地实现着*："结构性地"意味着这种破坏成为不可避免的，悲剧的是这种破坏也总是有害的——它构成了一种阶段性差异（phase difference），即*无法*在心理地和社会地个体化的意义上*被超个体化或被吸收*（在我看来，这似乎是尼克拉斯·卢曼［Niklas Luhmann］不能看到的）。

In other words, **this organological milieu poses in completely unprecedented terms the question of the relations between what Claude Bernard called the interior milieu and the exterior milieu.** *New conditions of fidelity are required in order to overcome the **shocks of infidelity**, so to speak, that* are **provoked by what I call the** *epokhally double redoubling*. This study of **milieus and infidelities** constitutes the field of what we can refer to as a general ecology inasmuch as it inscribes in the cosmos the perspectives of a general organology.

It is also the pathway to a new understanding of the dynamics and statics of religion.

换句话说，这种器官学的环境提出了一个前所未有的命题，这就是克洛德·贝尔纳（Claude Bernard）① 所说的内在环境和外在环境之关系的问题。需要新的忠诚条件来克服<u>背叛的冲击</u>（*shocks of infidelity*），而这就需要我所说的<u>二次中断重复</u>（*the epokhally double redoubling*）来激发。关于**环境和背叛性**的研究构成了**我们所说的一般生态学**的问题域，也标定了宇宙中的一般器官学视域。它也是对宗教的动力学和静力学进行新的理解的路径。

---

① 克洛德·贝尔纳（Claude Bernard, 1813—1878）：法国生理学家。历任法兰西学院生理学教授和胜利实验室主任（1852），法兰西科学院院士（1854），巴黎大学理学院生理学教授（1854—1868），法兰西科学院院长（1869）。1857年正式提出"内环境"概念。其代表作有：《实验医学导论》（1865）等。——译者注

5. *The quasi-causal economy of infidelity*
背叛的准-因果体系

  When **life** becomes **organological**, and not just organic, and **when the "external" technical milieu conditions and in so doing constitutes the interior milieu** of collective individuation and of the **social systems** in which it consists, as well as of **psychic individuation** (which results, as we now know, in **an organological re-organization of the organic organization** in which the **cerebral organ** primarily consists, and **through the psycho-synaptic internalization of the exosomatic and the social relations which it weaves**, as the work of Maryanne Wolf shows), organological and pharmacological beings encounter the infidelity of the technical milieu, which *as such* constitutes them as *noetic* beings, for whom <u>noesis is always both the repercussion (*contre-coup*) and the aftershock (*après-coup*) of an *epokhal technological shock*</u>.

当生命变成**器官学的**,而不是器官的,当"**外部的**"**技术环境决定和构成集体个体化的内部环境**,构成社会体系以及**心理个体化**的内部环境(我们知道,后者产生一种主要由**智力器官**组成的有机组织的器官学意义上的重组,正如玛丽安娜·沃尔夫 [Maryanne Wolf]① 在《普鲁斯特与乌贼:阅读如何改变我们的思维》 [*Proust and the Squid: The Story and Science of the Reading Brain*] 一书中所说的,这种重组主要是**通过社会关系和外在化关系的心理-联合内在化** [psycho-synaptic internalization] 而完成的)。器官学存在和药理学存在都会遭遇技术环境的背叛,而*同样地*,技术环境又将这些存在建构为**智性存在**(*noetic beings*)。对某些人来说,**认识活动**(**noesis**)**既是对一种时代性的技术休克的反应**(repercussion [*contre-coup*]),**也是对它的余悸**(aftershock [*après-coup*])。

Technological **shock** is **epokhal** in as much as **it makes an epoch**, that is, it is **a suspension, an interruption, a disruption, and as such** *stupefaction*. Epokhal technological shock (such as the thermodynamic machine in partnership with

---

① 玛丽安娜·沃尔夫(Maryanne Wolf):美国哈佛大学人类发展与心理学博士,美国塔夫茨大学艾略特-皮尔逊儿童研究与人类发展部教授,阅读与语言研究中心主任。其代表作有 *Proust and Squid: The Story and Science of the Reading Brain*. 中文版参见《普鲁斯特与乌贼:阅读如何改变我们的思维》,王惟芬、杨仕音译,中国人民大学出版社,2012年版。——译者注

discretization and the reproduction of the gestures of work by mechanical and automatic tertiary retention) is **stupefying** (and generates stupidity in a thousand ways) in **that it disrupts the organological arrangements established by a prior and metastabilized stage of transindividuation**—forming what Heidegger called "the **understanding** that being-there has of its being".

技术休克（Technological **shock**）是**时代性的**，因为**它塑造了一个新纪元**。也就是说，它是**一种悬置**（suspension）、**阻断**（interruption）、**中断**（disruption）**以及麻木**(*stupefaction*)。时代性的技术休克（比如热力机以及由机械的、自动的第三持存所造成的工作姿势的离散化和再生产）是**令人震惊的**（并产生各种各样的愚昧行为），**它扰乱了由先前的、亚稳定的**（metastabilized）**超个体化阶段所建立的器官学安排**——形成海德格尔所说的"彼在对其存在的**理解**"（the **understanding** that being-there has of its being）。

Such an "**understanding**" is **trans-individuated between the psychosomatic organs, technical organs and social organizations** (that Gille and Luhmann both call, but in two very different senses, "social systems"), and **engenders a new** "**understanding that being-there has of its being**" formed by the **new circuits of transindividuation** that form between **the initial technological shock and a second moment that amounts to a noetic fulfillment** (that is, a circuit of transindividuation) through which <u>stupor becomes surprise</u> and ultimately eventuates in an understanding.

这种"理解"就是**在心理器官、技术器官和社会组织之间所发生的超个体化**（吉尔和卢曼在两种不同的意义上将其称为"社会体系"），并通过**新**的超个体化循环而产生一种新的"**彼在对其存在的理解**"。这种新的超个体化循环**是在第一技术休克和第二环节之间形成的，而这种第二环节将积累成为一种智性完成**（noetic fulfillment）（即一种超个体化的循环），**由此<u>昏迷（stupor）变成惊讶</u>，并最终形成一种理解**（understanding）。

General ecology, general economy and general organology

GENERAL ECOLOGY
GENERAL ECONOMY
GENERAL ORGANOLOGY

are **attempts to form such circuits** in our epoch. This "generality" is indicative of **an attempt to respond to the generality (and to the planetary, and as such locally cosmic, globality) of** the shock *we are given to think*, and this requires us to **transform this thinking into action**, that is, into *decision*, a **decision that** *slices into* **becoming**, that **carves** *into* **it** in order to **carve** *out* a future, that is, **a protention that is** *desirable* **and that would not be reducible to becoming**: becoming, *devenir*, is **entropic**, whereas the **future**, *avenir*, is **negentropic**. Such a program is necessarily also a **neganthropology**.

NEGANTHROPOLOGY

一般生态学、一般经济学和一般器官学都试图在我们这个时代里形成这样的循环。这种"一般性"表明一种对我们要思考的休克的普遍性（以及对行星的 [**planetary**] 和地方性宇宙的 [**locally cosmic**] 整体性）作出反应的尝试，这要求我们将这种思考转变为行动，即作出*决断*，一种渗入生成的决断，一种刻入生成的决断，以便*创造出*一种未来，这是一种所欲求的前摄，而不能被简化为生成：生成（becoming, *devenir*）是熵的，而未来（future, *avenir*）则是**负熵**的。这样一个计划必然也是一种**负人类学**（**neganthropology**）。

Stupefaction, which is the **condition of noesis** (just as **stupidity** is the condition of **thinking**, as Nietzsche and

Deleuze say), **is that of which one always finds an echo,** more or less near or distant, in what I call **surprise,** a **sur-prised ap-prehension,** a *sur-prehension* (*surpréhension*), which would be **irreducible to under-standing**(*compréhension*), and where **this relates to reason, to that reason which Kant distinguished from understanding.**

麻木(*Stupefaction*) 是一种意识活动状态（就像尼采和德勒兹所说的，**愚昧是一种思考状态一样**），**是一个人总是能发现一种**或多或少、或远或近的**回声**（echo）**的状态**，我称之为**惊讶**（surprise），一种惊讶的恐惧（**sur-prised apprehension**），一种 *sur-prehension*（*surpréhension*）。它不可还原为**知性**（**under-standing** [*compréhension*]），而是**与理性有关，这个理性是康德将其与知性区分开来的理性。**

It is as *reconstitution of a fidelity to the milieu*, and, *in this milieu*, *to psychic individuals*, *technical individuals and social individuals* (via social systems), that **a** *libidinal economy in the sense* of Freud **is established that would also be a** *general* **economy and a general** *ecology*. In this libidinal and **as such** general economy, **psychic, technical and social individuals take care of one another through** *transductive* **relations,** relations in which one side (for example, psychic individuals) cannot exist without the others (for example, technical individuals or social individuals), even though **technical and social individuals *pre-cede* psychic individuals, and do so as the condition of formation of their *preindividual* funds, has shown in the book *L'individuation à la lumière des notions de forme et d'information* funds that were previously constituted as circuits of transindividuation for those who are now dead.**

作为一种对**环境的忠诚**以及在这种环境中对心理个人、技术个人和社会个人（通过社会体系）的忠诚的**重建，弗洛伊德意义上的力比多经济学**（*libidinal economy*）的建立也是**一种一般经济学和一般生态学**。在这种力比多经济学即一般经济学中，心理的、技术的和社会的个人通过**转导关系**（*transductive* relations）而关照彼此。在这种关系中，一方（比如心理个人）没有其他方面（比如技术个人或社会个人）就无法存在，即使技术个人和社会个人先于心理个人，因而是先于个人的基金（funds）的形成条件。在西蒙栋的《形式与信息概念中的个体化》（*L'individuation à la lumière des notions de forme et d'information*）一书中已经说明，这些基金是在此之前为那些现已经死去的人而建立的超个体化循环。

In principle, and because reason is rooted in what Kant called transcendental apperception as **the *spontaneous coming together that occurs between the noetic order and the cosmic order*, CARE, that is <u>Sorge</u>, insofar as it is inherently negentropic**, and as such derives from a neganthropology, is also that **care taken of ecology insofar as the cosmic milieu is locally neganthropic**

NEGANTHROPIC

and must be protected from anthropic disequilibriums.

ANTHROPIC DISEQUILIBRIUMS

原则上说，由于理性扎根于康德所说的先验统觉中，后者是**在智性规则和宇宙规则之间、与理性自发一起产生的**。**关涉（CARE，<u>Sorge</u>）在本质是负熵的**，同样地，也是源于一种负人类学（neganthropology）。**由于宇宙环境是局部负人的，且必须从人为的不平衡中摆脱出来，因此也需要对生态学进行关涉。**

In this sense where what geography calls anthropisation.

ANTHROPISATION

for example, **as anthroposiation of the see, leads, when it is not a special object for care, Sorge, to entropy that is destruction of the milieu.**

在这个意义上，地理学所说的人类化（anthropisation），比如作为看（see）的人类化，当它不是关涉（care，Sorge）的具体对象时，就会导致熵，即环境的破坏。

To what extent and in what economic conditions the coming together, the agreement, that founds **Kantian transcendental apperception is possible in the Anthropocene** epoch is the entire issue at stake in bringing together general ecology, general organology and general economy—libidinal economy as the possibility of **moving beyond the drive-based stage of consumerist capitalism** and as **constituting an economic system founded on the valorization of negentropy**

NEGENTROPY

translated into neganthropology.

NEGANTHROPOLOGY

在某种程度上，在相伴而生的经济状况中，有可能在人类纪中建立起康德式的先验统觉的同意（agreement）是随之而来的一般生态学、一般器官学和一般经济学中全部问题的关键——力比多经济学是**超越以驱力为基础的**（**drive-based**）消费资本主义阶段的一种可能性，也是建立一种基于由负熵向负人类学平稳过渡的经济体系的可能性。

The precedence of **technological shock** constitutes what Simondon described as **a *phase difference*** , and **it finds its point of departure in the *originary default of origin*** that is told in this text.

技术休克的优先性建构了西蒙栋所说的*阶段性差异*（a *phase difference*），它在*起源的原始缺陷*（*originary default of origin*）中找到了分离点（point of departure）。

In this regard, **the allegory of Prometheus and Epimetheus is the mythical formulation of what the archaeology of André Leroi-Gourhan describes as a process of exteriorisation**, after Canguilhem thought it as technical life, and that I myself call the pursuit of life, that is, of *negentropogenesis*

NEGENTROPOGENESIS

as an exosomatisation, that is, by means other than life.

在这一点上，**普罗米修斯和爱比米修斯的寓言就是安德烈·勒鲁瓦-古兰（André Leroi-Gourhan）的考古学所描述的外化过程的神秘形式**。康吉莱姆将其称为技术生命（technical life），我称之为生命的追求（the pursuit of life）——通过生命之外的手段而进行的、作为一种外在化的**负熵形成**（*negentropogenesis*）的追求。

This shock through which **life mortifies itself by secreting what I have described as an epiphylogenetic memory** that constitutes the possibility of what we today call **culture**, and which is **the unthought ground of what Dilthey called the science of spirit**, is also **what constitutes libidinal economy insofar as, as artefact, it constitutes the fetish and hence the organological body as object of desire**, as it was shown by Winnicott.

通过这种休克，生命由于隐藏我所说的后种系生成记忆（**epiphylogenetic memory**）而压抑自身，这种后种系生成**记忆构成了我们今天所说的文化**的可能性以及**狄尔泰在**

《精神科学中历史世界的建构》（*The Formation of the Historial World in the Human Sciences*）中所说的精神科学的无思性地基，而且也是构成力比多经济的东西，因为它作为人造物，将恋物癖和作为欲望对象的器官学意义上的身体建构为一种欲望对象，正如温尼科特（Winnicott）① 所展现的那样。

In this way, the **instinct** becomes the **drive**, that is, the capacity for **detachable fixations**, and this is the horizon of Arnold Gehlen in this work which is also to say, the capacity for **perversion**, and ultimately **desire**, via the binding of these drives through what Freud described as identification, idealization and sublimation, which is **always a neganthropic process**.

NEGANTHROPIC

通过这种方式，**本能**（**instinct**）变为**驱力**（**drive**），即**可拆分的固定物**的能力，这也是阿尔诺德·盖伦（Arnold Gehlen）在书中也提到的视域，即一种**颠倒**（**perversion**）的能力。最后，通过借助弗洛伊德所说的认同、理想化和

---

① 唐纳德·伍兹·温尼科特（Donald Woods Winnicott, 1896—1971）：英国精神分析学家，曾任英国精神分析协会主席（1956—1959/1965—1968）。其代表作有：《游戏和现实》（1982）、《成熟过程和促进性环境》（1988）等。——译者注

升华而将这些驱力捆绑在一起形成欲望的能力,而这总是一个负人类的过程。

Such a libidinal economy implements, through various causal chains arising from the cosmos and the biosphere, a positive quasi-causality, in the sense developed here by Deleuze.

这种力比多经济通过来自宇宙和生物圈的各种因果链而实行了一种积极的准-因果性(*positive quasi-causality*)。在这个意义上,德勒兹在《感觉的逻辑》(*Logique du Sens*)中发展了这种积极的准-因果性。

And as such **it inverts the arche-event of organological facticity into a therapeutic necessity**, and does so **to the benefit not only of psychic, technical and social individuals, but also vital, terrestrial and cosmic individuals**—to take care of psychic and collective individuation, that is, of the organological biosphere that we currently call the Anthropocene is *also* to take care of what constitutes the general ecological condition.

同样地,它将器官学的真实性的本原-事件

（arche-event）颠倒为一种治疗学的必要性，从而不仅有助于心理的、技术的和社会的个人，而且有助于有生命的、地球上的和宇宙中的诸个体：关涉心理的和集体的个体化，关涉我们目前所说的人类纪的器官学生物圈，也就是关涉那些构成一般生态条件的东西。

**SEVENTH COURSE
11 APRIL 2016**
/
Organology of Limits
and the Function of Reason

第 七 讲

2016.4.11

器官学的界限和理性的功能

6. Selection and decision
选择和决断

Last week, I proposed to articulate GEcology, GEconomy and GOrgano.

GENERAL ECOLOGY
GENERAL ECONOMY
GENERAL ORGANOLOGY

上周，我提到这些表达：GEcology，GEconomy 和 GOrgano。

I precise now that I conceive this arrangement as a libidinal economy being itself essentially a behaviour of care.

现在，我想明确将这些安排（arrangement）看作一种力比多经济学，它本身在本质上是一种关涉（care）行为。

The object of such an articulation is the process of

a negentropogenesis

NEGENTROPOGENESIS

specified as an **exosomatisation**, and that we should better write, then, **neganthropogenesis**.

具体来说,这种表达(articulation)所指称的是一种**外在化的负熵起源过程**(process of a negentropogenesis),而我们将其写为**负人类起源**(**neganthropogenesis**)应该更好一点。

It is here absolutely essential **to read and critique** *The German Ideology*, and then, **to re-read the** *Grundrisse* **on the basis of this re-reading of** *The German Ideology*, that I try to do myself here, in *States of Shock*, that is currently in translation in Chinese, that will be published by NUP, and where I comment this passage.

Nature builds no machines, no locomotives, railways, electric telegraphs, self-acting mules, etc. These are products of human industry; natural material transformed into organs of the human will over nature, or of human participation in nature. They are *organs of the human brain, created by the human hand*; the power of knowledge, objectified. The development of fixed capital indicates to what degree general social knowledge has become a *direct force of production*, and to what degree, hence, the conditions of the process of social life itself have come under the control of the general intellect and been transformed in accordance with it. To what degree the powers of social production have been produced, not only in the form of knowledge, but also as immediate organs of social practice, of the real life process.

这里，阅读和批判《德意志意识形态》是绝对重要的，基于对《德意志意识形态》的重读来重读《大纲》也是绝对重要的，我在《休克状态》(*States of Shock*) 中就是这样做的。目前这本书正在被译为中文，由南京大学出版社出版。在这本书中，我评论了马克思的这段话：

> 自然界没有造出任何机器，没有造出机车、铁路、电报、自动走锭精纺机，等等。它们是人的产业劳动的产物，是转化为人的意志驾驭自然界的器官或者说在自然界实现人的意志的器官的自然物质。它们是人的手创造出来的人脑的器官；是对象

化的知识力量。固定资本的发展表明，一般社会知识，已经在多么大的程度上变成了_直接的生产力_，从而社会生活过程的条件本身在多么大的程度上受到一般智力的控制并按照这种智力得到改造。它表明，社会生产力已经在多么大的程度上，不仅以知识的形式，而且作为社会实践的直接器官，作为实际生活过程的直接器官被生产出来。①

That is a kind of development of the first statements in *The German Ideology*：

Men can be distinguished from animals by consciousness, by religion or anything else you like. **They themselves begin to distinguish themselves from animals as soon as they begin to produce their means of subsistence**, a step which is **conditioned by their physical organisation.** By producing their means of subsistence men are **indirectly producing their actual material life.**

The way in which men produce their means of subsistence **depends** first of all **on the nature of the**

---

① 参见《马克思恩格斯全集》第 31 卷，人民出版社，1998 年版，第 102 页。——译者注

actual means of subsistence <u>they find in existence</u> **and have to reproduce**. This mode of production must not be considered simply as being the production of the physical existence of the individuals. Rather it is a definite form of activity of these individuals, a definite form of expressing their life, a definite mode of life on their part. **AS INDIVIDUALS EXPRESS THEIR LIFE, SO THEY ARE. What they are, therefore, coincides with their production, both with what they produce and with how they produce.** The nature of individuals thus depends on the material conditions determining their production.

我认为上述这段话是马克思对他在《德意志意识形态》中的第一次表述的发展：

可以根据意识、宗教或随便别的什么来区别人和动物。<u>一当人开始生产自己的生活资料</u>，即迈出由他们的肉体组织所决定的这一步的时候，<u>人本身就开始把自己和动物区别开来</u>。人们生产自己的生活资料，同时间接地生产着自己的物质生活本身。

人们用以生产自己的生活资料的方式，首先

取决于他们已有的和需要再生产的生活资料本身的特性。这种生产方式不应当只从它是个人肉体存在的再生产这方面加以考察。更确切地说，它是这些个人的一定的活动方式，是他们表现自己生命的一定方式、他们的一定的生活方式。个人怎样表现自己的生命，他们自己就是怎样。因此，他们是什么样的，这同他们的生产是一致的——既和他们生产什么一致，又和他们怎样生产一致。因而，个人是什么样的，这取决于他们进行生产的物质条件。①

As they express their life, so they are. With Marx, as Heidegger says, **being** becomes **production**. But such a production, that is also and first of all a **reproduction**, is **not simply an economy**: it is **the continuation of like as it is itself reproduction**—but this is **endosomatic**, whereas human reproduction is **exosomatic**.

他们怎样表现他们的生命，他们自己就是怎样。正如海德格尔说的，在马克思那里，**存在**变成了**生产**，而这个生产首先是**再生产**，不单是一种经济：它是一种正如它自

---

① 参见《马克思恩格斯文集》第 1 卷，人民出版社，2009 年版，第 519—520 页。——译者注

身的再生产一样的连续性——但是生产的再生产是**体内的**（**endosomatic**），而人类的再生产是**体外的**（**exosomatic**）。

And Georgescu-Roegen claims here that we must understand economy as a new law of relation between organs and of selection in a process of evolution, that is, as a bioeconomy, where exosomatic organs are detachable limbs, and they can create the possibility to exchange organs, hence these becoming goods in the sense of trade.

乔治斯库-罗根认为，我们必须将经济学理解为一种新的器官之间关系的规律和一种在进化过程中进行选择的规律，即理解为一种生物经济学（bioeconomy）。在这种经济中，体外器官是可分离的肢体，因而它们能创造出进行器官交换的可能性。因此，这些器官就变成了商业意义上的商品。

Only on the basis of such **a critique of what, in Marx and Engels, amounts to <u>the first philosophical formulation of the organological question</u>** (engendering and **preceding as it does the question of <u>class struggle</u>**), is it **possible and necessary to constitute general ecology on the basis of a general economy** (I continue here my discussion with Erich Hörl project), that is, a libidinal economy, itself conceived **on the basis of a general organology**, and is it possible and necessary to do so as a **new political thinking**, founded on **a critical reinterpretation of Marx, for example, concerning the dialectic of master and knecht**,

Work [...] is desire held in check, fleetingness staved off; in other words, work forms [...]. This [...] formative *activity* is at the same time the singularity [*die Einzelnheit*] or pure being-for-self of consciousness which now, in the work outside of it, acquires an element of permanence.

Hegel, *Phenomenology of Spirit*, § 195

只有基于对马克思和恩格斯的那种可归结为器官学问题的第一哲学公式的批判（器官学问题是产生和先于阶级斗争问题的），建立一种基于一般经济学（我会基于埃里希·霍尔的研究继续讨论这个问题）的一般生态学才是可能和必要的。这种一般经济学就是力比多经济学，它本身又是基于一般器官学的，作为一种新的政治思考来这样做是可能和必要的，这是基于对马克思的批判性重读而进行的——比如主-奴辩证法：

劳动是受到限制或节制的欲望，亦即延迟了的满足的消逝，换句话说，劳动陶冶事物……这个否定的中介过程或陶冶的行动同时就是意识的个别性或意识的纯粹自为存在，这种意识现在在劳动中外在化自己，进入到持久的状态。①

To inherit the Hegelian dialectic is, for Engels and Marx, firstly to inherit the dialectic of master and slave—itself founded on the dialectic of the *desire for recognition*. Now, that which leads to the dialectical inversion of the master by the slave, the latter having become "consciousness in itself and for itself", is, in Hegel, its pursuit of *knowledge*. That is, the slave achieves this inversion by the conquest of *determinations of the understanding*, and *by work*, by *putting technics to work*—the worker (who is the slave) gives himself an art, that is, a form of *knowledge* and an *individuation*, and ultimately a *property*, which *is* his individuation, that is, his existence *recognized*.

要继承黑格尔的辩证法，对马克思和恩格斯来说，首先是继承主-奴辩证法——它本身建立于*欲求认识的辩证法*

---

① 参见黑格尔：《精神现象学（上）》，贺麟、王玖兴译，商务出版社，1981年版，第130页。——译者注

(dialectic of the *desire for recognition*)。现在，使奴隶实现对主人的辩证颠倒，使奴隶变得具有自我意识的东西在黑格尔那里，就是对*知识*的追求。即奴隶是通过获得*理解的决断*，通过工作(*work*)，通过将技术用于工作而实现这种颠倒——工人（作为奴隶）给自己一种手艺（art），一种知识形式和一种个体化，最终获得一份财产（*property*），这是他的个体化，他的*被承认*的存在。

Now, this slave is not a slave, but a knecht, that is, a servant, and such a *knecht* is not at all a proletarian, if it is true that his dialectical and revolutionary power is based **on the increasing of his knowledge by work and by technical and technological practices**：he is **a craftsman**, that is a **future bourgeois**, whereas a proletarian is defined as **the one who has lost his knowledge**——this **knowledge** has **passed into the machine.**

现在，这个奴隶不再是奴隶，而是一个雇工（knecht），即一个仆人（servant）。这个*雇工不是无产者，他的辩证的革命的力量是***基于他通过工作、技能和技术的训练而真正地获得的知识的增长：他是一个工匠（craftsman），即未来的资产者（future bourgeois），***而无产者（proletarian）则被定义为*丧失了*知识的人——知识已经传递到机器中。

Work is *exteriorisation par excellence*, *that is*, *as individuation*, that is, **as exosomatisation**. As such, it is also **the exteriorisation of the for-itself of consciousness**—it is **the** *retaining of consciousness outside of itself*, *and the element of its permanence*—**his** *retention* is permanent only because it has become *tertiary*.

工作是**最典型的外化**（exteriorisation），即***个体化***，亦即**外在化**（exosomatisation）。同样地，它也是**意识*自为*的外化**（exteriorisation）：它将意识*保留*在自身之外，是意识***永存的环节***——意识的***持存***是永恒的，只是因为意识变为***第三性的***。

Through this **conquest of self in the exteriorisation of self**, and *for the master*, knecht consciousness achieves consciousness *in itself and for itself*, that is, *beyond* the master. And in the course of the moments of this dialectic,

> In the master, being-for-self is an "other" for the knecht, or is only *for* him (i. e. is not this own); in fear [that of the knecht who has become

the knecht through his recoil in the face of death, which the master does not fear, who as a result of this becomes the master], being-for-self is present in the knecht himself; in fashioning the thing [in the work imposed by **knechtschaft, servitude, as the stage of a *Bildung***], he becomes aware that being-for-self belongs to *him*, that he himself exists essentially and actually in his own right. **The shape does not become something other than himself through being made external (*hinausgesetzt*,** placed outside, as Hyppolite puts it, ***pros-thetized*** in some way) to him; for **it is precisely this shape that is his pure being-for-self, which in this externality is seen by him to be the truth.** Through this **rediscovery of himself by himself,** the knecht realizes that **it is precisely in his work wherein he seemed to have only an alienated existence that he acquires a mind of his own.**

    Hegel, *Phenomenology of Spirit* §196

  通过对自身外化的自我占有,对主人来说,雇工意识实现了*自我意识*,即*超越*主人的意识。这体现在这样的辩证过程中,在主人面前，奴隶感觉到自为存在只是外在的东西或者与自己不相干的东西；在恐惧中［雇工之所以成为雇工，是因为他面对死亡时的恐惧。而主人不畏惧死亡，因而成为主人］他感觉到自为存在只是潜在的；在陶冶事物的劳动中（在工匠、奴隶进行的工作即作为*教养*［***Bildung***］的阶段中），自为存在则属于*他自己固有*的了，并且他开始意识到他本身是自在自为地存在着的。奴隶据以陶冶事物的形式由于是客观地被建立起来的［正如伊波利特所做的那样，是以某种方式被置于外部］，因而对他并不是一个外在的东西，而即是他自身；因为这形式正是他的纯粹的自为存在，不过这个自为存在在陶冶事物的过程中才得到了实现。因此正是在劳动里（虽说在劳动里似乎仅仅体现异己者的意向），奴隶通过自己再重新发现自己的过程，才意识到他自己固有的意向。①

Actually, here, **Hegel says already what will be said by *The German Ideology* against… Hegel, that is, against idealism. Why? Because Hegel will say that this exteriorisation or externalisation is only a moment in a phenomenology of the**

---

① 参见黑格尔：《精神现象学（上）》，贺麟、王玖兴译，商务出版社，1981年版，第131页。译文有所改动。——译者注

spirit that will, having become absolute, **totally re-interiorize its previous exteriority.**

实际上，黑格尔所说的正是《德意志意识形态》所反对的，即反对黑格尔的唯心主义。为什么？因为黑格尔认为，这种外化或客观化是精神现象学中的一个环节，这个已经成为绝对的精神将**在总体上使它以前的外部再次内在化**。

This *dialectic of work and workers*, which is obviously the foundation of Marxism, in Hegel describes less the situation of the *worker becoming proletarian* than that of the *artisan becoming an entrepreneur*, that is, bourgeois. In other words, *the reappropriation of this dialectic by Marxism is based on a misunderstanding.*

显然，构成马克思主义之基础的<u>工作和工人的辩证法</u>，在黑格尔那里，并不是<u>工人变成无产者</u>的情况，而是<u>工匠</u>（*artisan*）<u>变为企业家</u>（*entrepreneur*）即资产者的情况。换句话说，马克思主义对这种辩证法的挪用是基于一种误解之上的。

Such a reinterpretation of Hegel and Marx is possible only on the basis of **a conjoined re-reading of Marx, Freud, Husserl, Heidegger, Canguilhem, Leroi-Gourhan, Derrida, Deleuze**, and many others, and of **Nicholas Georgescu-Roegen**—through **an investigation of the fundamental question of the difference between the organic and the organological**, which is also their mutual *différance(s)* with "a a",

DIFFÉRANCE (S)

and thereby opens **a new age of that *différance* that is <u>noesis</u>** (by tracing new circuits of transindividuation), in relation to the *différance* that is <u>life</u>.

这种对黑格尔和马克思的重新解读只有基于**对马克思、弗洛伊德、胡塞尔、海德格尔、康吉莱姆、勒鲁瓦-古兰、德里达、德勒兹、尼古拉斯·乔治斯库-罗根以及其他思想家进行重新阅读**才是有可能的——这是通过**对器官和器官学之间的差异**,亦即它们的带"a a"的相互*延异*(mutual *différance*[s])这一根本问题的研究来加以展开的,从而打开了一个与<u>生命延异</u>(the *différance* that is life) 相关的、(通过跟踪新的超个体化循环实现的)**认识**<u>延异</u>(*différance* that is <u>noesis</u>)的新阶段。

Such an investigation, such an instruction, is itself possible only by **adopting a method that will coordinate the diverse forms of knowledge** that constitute **the theory of general organology**, but that will also, and as organological practice, **invent <u>negentropic instruments</u>** at the service of **all forms of knowledge—savoir-faire, savoir-vivre, savoir-théoriser** (knowledge of how to do, live and theorize) —and that take the **digital** as its object insofar as 1. the digital is an affair of digits, that are fingers; 2. it is conceivable only on the condition of **rethinking all forms of knowledge starting from the organogenesis of artefacts, societies and psychic individuals** that has occurred since the origin of hominization.

这种研究和指导只有通过**采用协调不同形式的知识**这种方法才是可能的，这些知识构成了**一般器官学的理论**，它也将作为器官学实践，在**各种形式的知识**的辅助下**发明<u>负熵性的工具</u>**——这些知识包括**技能知识**（savoir-faire）、**生活知识**（savoir-vivre）和**理论知识**（savoir-théoriser）（即如何做的知识、如何生活的知识和如何理论化的知识）——将**数字化**作为它的对象，1. 只要这种数字化是手指的事情；2. 只有<u>重新反思自人类演化起源以来已经发生的从人造物到社会再到心理个人的器官发生所形成的各种形式的知识</u>，这才是可能的。

Until big data under the data economy, and, even beyond, as medicine 3.0 and at the end this new stage of exosomatisation that Transhumanism is the ideology, that is, also, the strategic marketing in the disruption of the rules of life itself, some people claiming that through this, Google becomes totalitarian, and where the question of fingers as digits is anew put out and in a new perspective, that is for me the one of the Anthropocene and the bifurcation we must provoke in it, so opening the possibility of the Neganthropocene.

直到数据经济①下的大数据，甚至到达药3.0和这种外

---

① "数据经济（Data Economy）"是一个新兴的互联网经济概念。它是随着互联网技术的快速发展和物联网经济的普及而产生的以数据为基础的新型产业经济形态。企业或机构通过对海量数据进行采集、精炼、分析、处理和存储来提升经营效率、制定战略决策，设计创新性产品、服务和商业模式，以全方位满足消费者需求，获取巨大经济效益。——译者注

在化的新阶段的终点，超人类主义（Transhumanism）① 都是一种意识形态，也就是在生命本身的规律发生中断时产生的战略性的市场营销。有些人宣称借助这种意识形态，谷歌将变成极权主义（totalitarian），于是作为数字（digits）的手指问题就再次出现了。从一个新的角度来看，它对我来说就是一个人类纪以及我们在其中必须激起的转折点（bifurcation），这样一来才能打开通向逆人类纪的可能。

*

As I can imagine it, the **general ecology** invoked by Erich Hörl is **both a scientific and a political ecology**, and it must as such **tightly articulate** the **questions of selection and of decision** —in the epoch of the **digital trace** and its **algorithmic treatment**, as well as **in debate with Nietzsche**. It is, in other

---

① 超人类主义（Transhumanism）：英文缩写为 H+，又译为超人文主义、超人主义、过渡人文主义等。它是一个通常用来表示人类增强的术语，目前已形成一个国际性的文化智力运动，支持发展和利用科学技术来改善人类状况，即增强人类的身体、精神和心理等能力，克服人类社会的贫困、疾病、残疾等状况，并寻求建立平等和谐的社会体系，追求人类福祉。在超人类主义思想史上，最早可追溯到古希腊哲学家苏格拉底，近代早期超人类主义者包括阿利盖利·但丁、朱利安·赫胥黎、J. B. S. 霍尔丹和 FM-2030。马克斯·莫（Max More）第一个完整定义了超人类主义，尼克·博斯特罗姆和大卫·皮尔斯于 1998 年创立世界超人协会。超人类主义在发展过程中也形成了不同流派，主要包括：民主超人类主义、快乐主义、奇点主义（Singularitarianism）、理论超人类主义、沙龙超人类主义等。虽然超人类主义不断受到其他思想流派的批判，但不可否认的是它对文学、电影、音乐、政治等众多领域产生了广泛影响。——译者注

words, a fundamental critique that poses the question of the *criteria of selection*, formed in such a way that they become criteria *of decision*, that is, critical CATEGORIES rather than merely biological, psychic or technical automatisms.

我能够想象，埃里希·霍尔所呼吁的一般生态学既是一种科学的生态学，也是一种政治的生态学。同样地，它必须紧紧围绕选择问题和决断问题——在这个充满数字踪迹及其算法处理的时代，同样也在与尼采的争论中进行。换句话说，这个根本的批判提出了选择标准的问题，同样变成了决断即批判性范畴（critical CATEGORIES）的标准，而不仅仅是生物学的、心理的或技术自动主义的标准。

The *passage* from *psycho-biological automatic selection* to its *disautomatization* as DECISION is possible only when *organic* organs combine with, and form a *system* with the organological organs that are tertiary retentions, that is, with the epiphylogenetic supports of collective memory, opening up an *interpretative play* (a *différance*) through which criteria of selection become criteria of decision, that is, of psychosocial individuation, and not just vital individuation.

从心理-生物学的自动选择向作为决断的去自动化的转

变只有在以下这种情况下才成为可能，即当*有机器官*与*作为第三持存的器官学的器官*联合起来并组成一个系统时，当有机器官与集体记忆的后种系生成支撑（epiphylogenetic supports）联合在一起时，而这种集体记忆会打开一种*解释性剧本*（一种延异），借助这种解释性剧本，选择的标准就变为决断的标准，即社会心理的个体化的标准，而不只是生命个体化的标准。

The outcome of this interpretative play is the **production of circuits of transindividuation**, that is, the continuous formation **of new knowledge**—such as thermodynamic emerging from the steam machine —arising from the unfurling of organogenesis, generating new *pharmaka* from the circuits of transindividuation, deriving from constituted knowledge, in turn requiring new forms of knowledge placing into crisis those from which they stem, and **provoking more or less stupefaction from this *pharmakon*** that is **always stunning and astounding**. Now, here, **artificial intelligence seems to be a limit**. But in what extent?

这种解释性剧本的结果就是超个体化循环的产生，即不断形成新的知识——比如来自蒸汽机的热力学——这种新知识产生于器官形成的展开，并在超个体化的循环中产生新的*药*，同时产生于已形成的知识。反过来，需要将各种形式的新知识置入它们要阻止的危机之中，这些总是美妙的、惊人的*药*会产生或多或少的麻木。现在，在这一点上，人工智能似乎是一种极限。但这是什么程度上的极限呢？

Hence is produced the transformation **of techno-epokhal shock into a surprise, a sur-prehension** that eventually becomes a com-prehension, which is **less the understanding** that being-there has of its being than **that through which psychosocial individuation takes care of its organological and pharmacological condition**, as "Sorge", by **trans-forming** *technical becoming* at a single stroke into a *noetic future*, **that is, into the** *desire to live in quasi-causality*, in the sense of Deleuze, and therefore *by default*, and **as a default** *that is necessary*—and on the basis of which, and because it has become banal, can arise **a new and always surprising pharmacology.**

由此，技术-时代性休克转变为一种惊讶（surprise），一种 sur-prehension，最终变为一种 com-prehension——这不是彼在对其存在的<u>理解</u>，而是<u>对借此社会心理的个体化关涉它的器官学的、药理学的状况的理解，就像通过将单向*技术生成*变为一种智性未来即生活在德勒兹意义上的准-因果性中的欲望而实现</u>的"关涉（Sorge）"。因此，通过*缺陷*(*default*)，**作为一种必然的缺陷**——并基于这种缺陷，因为它已经变得平庸，就能够产生一种新的、总是令人惊讶的药理学。

7. Neganthropy of "torpor" —*if not stupor, if not stupidity*

"迟钝"的负人类——如果没有麻木,如果没有愚昧

It is in the context of this normativity that we must interpret **Canguilhem** when he posits that **knowledge of life is the specific form of life capable of caring for itself, treating itself**, particularly as biology, —and, in the same way, **we must understand ecology as this same form of life caring for itself through the knowledge of the milieus, systems and processes of individuation** through which the **concrescence of the cosmos** generates processes of individuation such that entropic and negentropic tendencies play out in different ways in each of the different forms of infidelity of these milieus.

在这种规范性的语境中,我们必须解读**康吉莱姆**,当他提出生命知识就是考察那些能够关涉自身、料理自身的

特殊生命形式，生物学尤为如此——同样地，我们必须将生态学理解为生命关涉自身的同样的形式，这种关涉是通过个体化的环境、系统和过程的知识实现的，由此宇宙的合生（concrescence of the cosmos）产生了个体化的过程，从而熵的和负熵的趋势以不同方式在每一种不同形式的环境背叛中发挥出来。

The questions about **life and negentropy** that arise with Darwin and with thermodynamics must in this sense be reinterpreted in the **organological context**, given that **natural selection gives way to artificial selection**, and that the passage from **the organic to the organological displaces the play of entropy and negentropy**.① Thought in this way, **technics is an** *accentuation of negentropy*, since it is a **factor of** *increased differentiation*, but it is *also* an *acceleration of entropy* — not just because it is a process of combustion and of the dissipation of energy, but because *industrial standardization* seems today to lead to the destruction of life as the burgeoning and proliferation of differences: biodiversity, cultural diversity and the singularity of psychic individuations as

---

① Which cannot but radically affect ecological science, and not just political ecology. But it does so by inscribing the political event into the very heart of the science of the living in its negotiation with the organized non-living and the organizations in which it results.

well as collective individuations——and this is what one calls Anthropocene.

  既然自然选择为人为选择打开了通道,既然从器官的向器官学的转变代替了熵和负熵的作用①,那么,来自达尔文和热力学的关于**生命和负熵**的问题就必须在**器官学的语境(organological context)** 中进行重新解读。沿着这一思路,技术就是一种**对负熵的强化(accentuation of negentropy)**,因为它是导致分化不断增加的一个因素,但它同时也是一种**对熵的加速(acceleration of entropy)**——不仅因为这是一个能量消耗的燃烧过程,也因为今天工业的标准化似乎导致生命的破坏,即快速发展和扩散的差异:生物多样性,文化多样性及心理个体化和集体个体化的独特性——这就是所谓的人类纪。

  Only from this perspective do the questions of *Bestand*, *Gestell* and *Ereignis* make sense for us——for those in the Anthropocene who question the epokhal singularity in which this time, which is a period that presents itself as the probability of the end of time, fails to consist, so to speak. But if so,

---

  ① 这种变化会彻底影响到生态科学,而不只是会影响政治生态学。但是,这种影响是通过将政治事件嵌入生活科学的核心而实现的,这种生活与有组织的非生活及其组织处于协商状态。

Bestand, *Gestell* and *Ereignis* take on a meaning that is in a way the epoch of the default of epoch, which is possible only according to a twist of meaning that is incompatible with Heideggerian thought—even less so given that **the epokhal dimension of thermodynamics is in no way taken into account in the writings of the *Kehre*.**

只有从这个角度，持存、座架和生成问题对我们才是有意义的，也就是说，对那些在人类纪中追问这个时代的时代独特性（epokhal singularity）的人们来说才是有意义的，这个时代呈现出一个自身时代终结的可能性，一个无法持续下去的阶段。如果是这样，那么持存、座架和生成就具有了一种在某种程度上揭示这个具有时代缺陷的时代的意义，而这只有根据一种与海德格尔思想相对立的意义的扭转才有可能——更不用说，**热力学的时代性维度在海德格尔思想转向（Kehre）的著作中还没有被考虑到。**

In addition, the *perspective and the prospect* (that is, the future) that I propose here (as the epoch still to come) in terms of general organology with respect to a Neganthropocene calling upon **a neganthropological conception of noetic life, that is, of life that studies and knows life in order to care for it** (as biology, ecology, economy, organology and everything that this entails, namely, every form of **knowledge** understood in terms of its **cosmic tenor**), is also functionally and primordially that of a **libidinal economy,** and of such an economy **rethought in organological terms and as general economy in Georges Bataille's sense,** that is, as we will see, an **economy of gift,** that is of **potlatch,** this **general economy** requiring a **complete redefinition of phenomenology** in general and the **existential analytic** in particular.

除此之外，根据与逆人类纪相关的一般器官学，我对*未来图景的建议*是倡导一种负人类学意义上的智性生命观（**conception of noetic life**），即研究和了解生命以便关涉生命（比如生物学、生态学、经济学、器官学及与此相关的任何学科，即根据**宇宙规律**来理解每一种**知识形式**）。这种观念在功能上和本真性上也是一种**力比多经济学**观念，重新思考这种器官学的意义上的经济学和巴塔耶意义上的一般经济学。我们将看到，这种一般经济学是一种礼物经济学（**economy of gift**），一种赠礼性的经济学（**economy of potlatch**）。这种一般经济学需要给予一种彻底的一般现象学的重新定义和特殊的**存在论分析**。

Such a redefinition passes through the inscription of Freudian shock within an organological perspective, thereby going **beyond Freud himself.** It means asking the organological question of **tertiary retention** as that which constitutes the possibility of the **dis-automatization of instinct**—in a vein not foreign to the questions raised by Arnold Gehlen, who must be read here with John Bowlby and Donald Winnicott. The **dis-automatization of instinct** comes at the cost of the **formation of other automatisms**, artificial—psychic, technical and social—automatisms, that as a general rule require an economy, that which sets the rules in any society and does so through various forms of regulation (rituals, education, law, institutions) governing the processes of exchange resulting from the dis-automatization of the instincts insofar as this makes possible and necessary the detachability of artificial organs, becoming objects of exchange, as well as the **detachability of the drives, which, precisely insofar as they themselves become detachable, must be bound together so as not to become entropic,** this constituting the horizon of *Beyond the Pleasure Principle* as the dimension of death drive into noetic life.

这种再定义需要通过从器官学视域出发标定弗洛伊德式的震惊（Freudian shock）来完成，由此也**超越了弗洛伊德**。这意味着要追问器官学的**第三持存**问题，而这种第三持存构成了**本能的去自动化**(dis-automatization of instinct)的可能性——在某种意义上,这并不异质于阿尔诺德·盖伦(Arnold Gehlen)① 所提出的问题,而必须结合约翰·鲍比(John Bowlby)② 和唐纳德·温尼科特(Donald Winnicott)来阅读他。这种**本能的去自动化**是以**其他自动主义**,人为的——即心理的、技术的和社会的——自动主义**的形成**为代价的,后者作为普遍规律需要一种经济学。这种经济学将规律置入任何一种社会中,通过各种形式的规则(仪式、教育、法律、机构)来管理由本能的去自动化而产生的交换过程,本能的去自动化使人造器官可分,从而使人造器官变成交换的对象成为可能。同样地,**本能的去自动化**也使驱力的可分,准确地说,这使驱力本身变成可分的成为可能。但这些可分的驱力和人造器官必须结合在一起才不会变为熵的。这构成了《超越快乐原则》(*Beyond the Pleasure Principle*)的视域,即从死亡驱向智性生命的维度。

General economy, general ecology and general

---

① 阿尔诺德·盖伦(Arnold Gehlen,1904—1976):德国哲学家、社会学家、哲学人类学。曾任教于法兰克福大学、柯尼斯堡大学、维也纳大学和阿亨工业大学。其代表作有:《道德与超道德:一种多元主义伦理学》(1969)等。——译者注

② 约翰·鲍比(John Bowlby,1907—1990):英国发展心理学家,提出依恋理论。其代表作有:《依恋》(1969/1982)、《安全基础》(1988)等。——译者注

organology are **a salvage effort with respect to the conditions of a libidinal economy today ruined**, which it is a matter of **rethinking from the perspective of neganthropology starting from the fetish, the transitional object and the artefact** as condition of all **consistence** beyond subsistence and existence (in the sense I explained in the first lecture) —and in the sense where **Whitehead inscribes this dimension of consistence at the heart of concrescence.**

一般经济学、一般生态学和一般器官学是**挽救今天被毁坏的力比多经济条件的一种努力，这就是从始于恋物（fetish）的负人类学角度进行的重新思考，这种恋物是一种过渡性对象和**作为超越了生计（subsistence）和生存（existence）（在我在第一讲中所解释的意义上）的一切**持存**（**consistence**）条件的人造物——在这个意义上，**怀特海将持存的维度标定为共生的核心**。

General economy, ecology and organology thus conceived with Georges Bataille, together call for **Vladimir Vernadsky's concept of "biosphere"**, later replaced with that of **"global ecosystem"**, and reactivated in France by René Passet, a concept with which we can explore **the paradox of technology**, which is another name for what Ivan Illich called

counterproductivity. When, *as a system*, the growth of technology reaches a certain point, its *effects are inverted*, and as such it becomes paradoxical, which Passet described as a **"passage to limits"**. We must **relate this concept of counterproductivity to the *pharmakon*** in general, and the diverse counterproductive effects of the prevailing organological condition should be seen as **entropic and negentropic pharmacological effects.**

由乔治·巴塔耶提出的一般经济学、生态学和器官学，共同呼吁弗拉基米尔·维纳德斯基（Vladimir Vernadsky）[①]的"生物圈"概念，后者被"全球生态系统（global ecosystem）"概念所取代，而在法国则由雷内·帕赛特（René Passet）[②]重新激活。借助这个概念我们可以研究**技术的矛盾（paradox of technology）**，这就是伊万·伊里奇（Ivan Illich）[③]所说的**逆生产力**（counterproductivity）。当技术作为体系发展到某一点，它的效果就会发生颠倒，同样地，它

[①] 弗拉基米尔·维纳德斯基（Vladimir Vernadsky, 1863—1945）：俄国与乌克兰矿物学家、地球化学家，地球化学、生物地球化学和放射地质学的奠基者之一。获得斯大林奖（1943）。其代表作有：《生物圈》（1926）等。——译者注

[②] 雷内·帕赛特（René Passet, 1926— ）：法国经济学家，法国索邦大学荣誉教授，课征金融交易税以协助公民组织（ATTAC）委员会主席。其代表作有：《经济与生活》（1979）等。——译者注

[③] 伊万·伊里奇（Ivan Illich, 1926—2002）：奥地利哲学家、社会学家、罗马天主教神父。其代表作有：《去学校化社会》（1971）、《陶然自得的工具》（1973）等。——译者注

就变得具有矛盾性，帕赛特（Passet）将其描述为"**趋向极限的过渡（passage to limits）**"。我们必须将逆生产力这个概念与一般的**药**联系起来，一般器官学状况的各种逆生产性效果应该被看作熵的和负熵的药理学效果。

The **automotive** *pharmakon*, the car, created to augment mobility, engenders urban congestion. The **computerized** *pharmakon*, created to *assist with decision-making*, engenders **cognitive overflow syndrome and paralysis** (confounded with **stupefaction** and consolidated with the **systemic and functional stupidity** wrought by **drive-based capitalism**, to which is added, in France, the **institutional stupidity** generated by the **Ecole Nationale d'Administration**, an institution responsible for training, for example, François Hollande and most of his advisers. Hence France hurtles towards its current fate, one in which stupidity reaches extreme levels).

机动性的药即汽车，提高了流动性，也产生了城市拥堵。**计算机化的药**，一方面能**辅助决策**，另一方面产生了**认知上的综合病症和瘫痪**（困扰于**麻木**，受困于**基于驱力的资本主义**所导致的**系统性和功能性愚昧**，甚至在法国还有由**国家行政学院**［Ecole Nationale d'Administration］所产生的**制度性愚昧**，这个机构负责向总统弗朗西斯·奥朗德和他的顾问提供培训,因此法国奔向了它现在的命运,愚昧达到了最极端的程度)。

This paradox can also be seen with *medicines* **that, if poorly prescribed** (not just in the wrong doses), **poison the patient**, or may even produce what in pharmaceutical science is called a **"paradoxical reaction"**, that is, where the medicine acts in such a way that it causes the very thing against which it is intended to fight.

这种矛盾在药上也能看到,如果处方不对的话(不只是在于剂量错误),就会对患者造成毒害,甚至产生在制药科学中所谓的"矛盾反应(paradoxical reaction)",即药物发挥了与它应发挥的效应相反的作用。

The **pharmacological paradox** equally afflicts the **social organizations** that are institutions and corporations insofar as they always make use of political technologies, governmentality and management, in the sense in which Foucault placed these **political technologies** at the heart of his thought of power in general under the umbrella of biopower (which should be related back to Weber, and read alongside Polanyi), an issue that should also be explored with Gille and

Luhmann with respect to the concept of social system, all of these things constituting **specific cases of the pharmacology that conditions and limits any organology** and therefore any human ecology.

这种**药理学的矛盾**同样适用于作为机构和团体的**社会组织**，他们总是利用**政治技术**、治理术和管理。在这个意义上，福柯将政治技术放在了其生命权力下的普遍权力思想的核心地位（这可以回溯到韦伯，以及结合波兰尼来阅读），这个问题也要结合吉尔和卢曼的社会系统概念来研究，所有这些都构成了**药理学的具体方面，药理学决定和限制任何器官学**和人类生态学。

8. Limits
界限

We must, then, also examine more closely the **general conditions of emergence of these paradoxical effects**, and we must do so alongside a reading of Passet's *L'Économique et le Vivant*, in which the problem of **sustainable development** is examined from the perspective of **systems theory**, in terms of **passages to limits** in various domains, domains that are understood as systems or elements of systems.

Sustainable development is not a question like others, or just one among others. This question reveals a passage to limits through which it is **the interplay of economic laws** that **is transformed.**

我们需要进一步研究这些矛盾效应产生的一般条件,并同时阅读帕赛特的《经济与生命》(*L'Économique et le*

Vivant)。在这本书中，根据各个系统的或系统要素所经历的**界限**，可持续发展问题被从**系统论**的角度研究了：

> 可持续发展不是一个与其他问题相同的问题，或者不是一个与其他问题并存的问题。这个问题揭示了通向极限的过程，在这一过程中，经济规律的相互作用被改变了。

These limits raise the question of **new equilibriums and disequilibriums**, establishing **new general conditions of <u>intersystemic metastability</u>**.

> Beginning in the eighties, in fact, with the issue of global damage to the biosphere…, **it is no longer specific resources or environments that are threatened, but the regulatory mechanisms of the planet itself.**

这些界限产生了**新的均衡和非均衡**的问题，建立起<u>系统间的亚稳定性</u>（intersystemic metastability）的新的一般条件：

> 实际上，在 20 世纪 80 年代初，随着全球范

围内生物圈遭受破坏问题的出现，不再是个别的资源或环境受到威胁，而是这个星球本身的规则机制受到了威胁。

The **biosphere** is defined here, following Vladimir Vernadsky, as **a complex and self-regulating system, in the adjustments and evolutions of which life**—and thus the human species—**plays a fundamental role**. Two logics confront each other here, that which presides over the **development of economic systems** and that which ensures the **dynamic reproduction of natural environments**.

这里的**生态圈**是随着弗拉基米尔·维纳德斯基（Vladimir Vernadsky）将其定义为一种**复杂的自我调节的系统**，它**在生命**——包括人类——**的调整和进化中发挥了根本性的作用**。这里存在两条逻辑：掌控**经济体系发展**的逻辑和保证**自然环境的动态再生产**的逻辑。

The question raised here is that of the Anthropocene—more than twenty years before its more or less official recognition—at the level of **natural milieus**. But this question also arises today, and perhaps especially, and certainly *firstly*, at the level of **organological milieus** *themselves*, and of *social* *systems and social environments*, that is, **mental environments** in the supposedly knowledge society.

这里就出现了人类纪问题——20多年前这个问题或多或少被官方认识到——在**自然环境**层面上的人类纪问题。然而，这个问题在今天也出现了，而且是首次在**器官学环境**层面上和在社会体系和社会环境，即在假设性的知识社会中的**精神环境**层面上出现了。

For if it is true that **the question is care, its organization, its culture**, one might even say its **worship** [*culte*], and **as the formation of attention through circuits of transindividuation that cultivate reason through reasons to live and to take care of life in quasi-causality**, *then* **the question of mental ecology precedes the question of environmental economy** —even though mental ecology is conditioned by organology and pharmacology, so that from Plato to Marx and up until ourselves, it presents itself as the question of *stupor*, or of *torpor*. I employ this latter term that Adam Smith used in his analysis of the extremes of the industrial division of labour — "torpor" was used by Smith to describe the **effects of mechanization on the minds** of those who were in the course of becoming proletarian.

因为如果这个问题能够在社会组织、文化甚至崇拜（**worship**［*culte*］）中获得真正的对待，随着注意力通过借助生活理性和在**准-因果性**中关涉生命的理性来陶冶理性的超个体化循环而形成，那么，<u>精神生态学问题就将优先于环境经济学问题</u>——即使精神生态学是以器官学和药理学为条件的。因此，从柏拉图到马克思再到我们，精神生态学都表现为**昏迷**（*stupor*）或**迟钝**（*torpor*）的问题。我用的第二个术语是亚当·斯密在分析工业的劳动分工所造成的极端状况时所使用的术语——"迟钝"被斯密用来描述**机械化**对<u>那些正变成无产者的人</u>的**思想所造成的影响**。

And such **torpor** becomes, in our time, a **stupor** —and our stupefaction in the face of the state of shock provoked by digital technology leads not only to functional stupidity, but to a catastrophic and dis-astrous（losing the light of the stars, the stars that in French are "asters", and losing them <u>for lack of a **therapeutic of computation** based on a new cosmology</u>），［a catastrophic and dis-astrous］<u>**destruction of** *noesis* **itself**</u> by automatic proletarianization.

在我们时代，这种**迟钝**（**torpor**）变成一种**昏迷**（**stupor**）——我们在面对数字技术引发的休克状态时所产生的麻木（stupefaction）不仅导致功能性愚昧（functional stupidity），而且导致由**自发的无产阶级化所引起的一种灾难性的、悲剧性的**（即丧失了星光，这是因为缺乏基于一种新宇宙学的**计算疗法**）**认识本身的毁灭**。

As for development, in Passet's terms, this involves growth that is both complexifying and multi-dimensional,
- this growth is complexifying through a **dual movement of diversification and integration**, allowing the system to grow by **reorganizing itself yet without losing its coherence**;
- it is multi-dimensional to the extent that, **beyond the economic in the strict sense**, it takes into account **the quality of the relations established between human beings** within the human sphere, and **their relations with the natural environment.**

至于发展，在帕赛特（Passet）看来，它包含了既错综复杂又多重维度的增长：
・这种增长通过**多样化和一体化的双重运动**而变得错综复杂，这种双重运动使系统能通过**认识自身而不丧失自己的一致性**而获得增长；
・它的多维性是**就严格意义上的超越经济学**而言，它要考察的是在人类领域中**人与人的关系的质量**以及**人与自然环境之间的关系**。

This duality is a source of conflict because while **nature maximizes its stocks (biomass) on the basis of a given flow (solar radiation)**, the **economy maximizes market flow by depleting natural (non-market) stocks**, the **decrease** of which is noted in **no economic records** and produces no corrective action.

这种两重性是一种冲突的来源,因为当**自然基于一个既定的流(太阳辐射)而使它的容量(生物量)达到最大时,经济则通过减少自然(非市场)容量而使市场流达到最大,自然容量的减少在非经济的记录中**被注意到,并产生了非正确的行动。

Hence there arises a question of nature and culture. I would have liked to show that to address Passet's question we must overcome this opposition, but I will be able to do no more than give an outline of this in my concluding remarks.

这就带来了一个自然和文化的问题。我想说,为了应对帕赛特(Passet)所提出的问题,我们必须克服它的对立面,但我只能给出一个提纲性的总结评论。

Be that as it may, this conflict has today reached a

threshold that amounts, precisely, to a passage to limits. Now, in reaching its limits, any system in **"phase transition"** undergoes **changes in the way it functions**

• the limit of the **saturation of needs**…
• the limit of the **reproducibility of a natural resource**…
• the limit of **rhythms of assimilation and self-purification**…①

或许，这种冲突在今天已经达到一种界域（threshold），准确地说，这种界域通向各种界限。现在，在通向各种界限的过程中，在"阶段性过渡"中的任何系统都将**按照它起作用的方式发生变化**：

• 需求饱和的界限……
• 自然资源可再生性的界限……
• 同化和自净化节律的界限……②

Such a passage to limits is a **sudden return to entropy**. At stake is therefore the power **to provoke bifurcations** in this

---

① René Passet (1996) *L'Économique et le Vivant*. Paris: Economica, pp. x-xii.
② René Passet (1996) *L'Économique et le Vivant*. Paris: Economica, pp. x-xii.

entropic becoming, reopening **unknown pathways to come, to the future**—and I argue (in agreement, I think, with the perspective of Erich Hörl) that **such pathways are organological**, and must above all consider the still **unknown possibility of the most recent stage of grammatization**, that is, of **digital tertiary retention** inasmuch as it makes possible **new and unprecedented neganthropic works**.①

NEGANTHROPIC WORKS

这种通向极限就是**突然返回到熵**。因此，在这个过程中，力量（power）**在熵的生成中产生很多分叉点（bifurcations）**，这些分叉点重新打开了**通向未来的未知路径**——我认为（我同意埃里希·霍尔的观点）**这些路径是器官学的**，而且必须考虑到**编程化的最近阶段的未知可能性**，这种编程化也就是**数字第三持存**，它使新的、前所未有的负人类的（neganthropic）工作成为可能。②

The latter pass through a **fundamental economico-political change**, which takes account of **automation** and its **ruinous effects on employment**, and installs **a new mechanism**

---

① These perspectives are developed in Bernard Stiegler (2015) *La Société automatique 1. L'avenir du travail*. Paris: Fayard.
② 关于这些观点的发展，请参见：Bernard Stiegler (2015) *La Société automatique 1. L'avenir du travail*. Paris: Fayard.

to redistribute productivity gains, in the wake of the analyses of Oskar Negt and André Gorz, in the form of time allocated for the **development of individual and collective capabilities** (in Amartya Sen's sense). It is for this reason that Ars Industrialis advocates the creation of a **contributory revenue**, modelled on the law of the **"intermittents" of the artistic sphere in France**, and IRI is developing contributing research platforms with a view to designing a new architecture of the world wide web at the service of an economy that values negentropy and fights entropy at the same time.

后者将经历一场根本性的经济-政治变革，这场变革不仅涉及自动化及其对就业的破坏性影响，而且根据奥斯卡·内格特（Oskar Negt）[1]和安德烈·高兹（André Gorz）[2]的分析，它还会建立一种新的机制来重新分配生产成果，而这种分配是以时间在个人能力和集体能力（在阿玛蒂亚·桑［Amartya Sen］[3]的意义上）发展中的分配的

---

[1] 奥斯卡·内格特（Oskar Negt，1934— ）：德国著名社会学家，法兰克福学派代表人物之一。曾任汉诺威大学社会学教授。其代表作有：《康德与马克思》（2003）、《政治的人：作为生活方式的民主》（2010）等。——译者注

[2] 安德烈·高兹（André Gorz，1923—2007）：法国左翼思想家、《新观察家》周刊的创始人。其代表作有：《历史的道德》（1959）、《社会主义与革命》（1967）等。——译者注

[3] 阿马蒂亚·库马尔·森（Amartya Kumar Sen，1933— ）：著名福利经济学家，诺贝尔经济学奖获得者（1998），现任哈佛大学经济学和哲学教授、托马斯·W. 拉蒙特大学教授，曾任剑桥大学三一学院院长（1998—2004）。其代表作有：《贫困和饥饿：论权力和剥夺》（1981）等。——译者注

形式而展开的。正是因为这个原因，精神技术工业政治国际联合会（Ars Industrialis）倡导创造一种**贡献性收入（contributory revenue）**，以法国艺术界的"**临时工（intermittents）**"法律为模型，蓬皮杜艺术中心研究与创新学院（IRI）正在开发一种贡献性研究平台，在一种看重负熵、反对熵的经济的辅助下，设计一种新的万维网结构。

These perspectives are developed in my two last books and I will return to these questions in the next session.

这些观点在我最近的两本书中得到进一步发展。我将在下节课再回到这些问题。

9. *The calculation industry, quantum organization of the inorganic, and decision*
计算工业、无机物的量子组织以及决断

Let us conclude by turning to **Whitehead.** When he introduces the **concept of process,** he at the same time establishes that **the *opposition* between natural phenomena and cultural phenomena has become out-dated.** This obviously does not mean that the *distinction* between nature and culture would be out-dated. In this way, a general economy is outlined that is not yet a general organology, but that calls for the latter and requires it.

让我们回到**怀特海**。当他引入**过程概念**时,他同时指出**自然现象和文化现象的对立已经过时了**。这显然不是说,自然和文化之间的*区分*过时了。这样,一种一般经济学就被勾勒出来,却还不是一种一般器官学,但是前者呼唤并且需要后者。

In Whitehead, with regard to **cosmology**, it **is no longer a question of spheres, but of process**, that is, more precisely, of **dynamic interlocked spirals materialized by regimes of speed** —and **where there is such a thing as** *infinite speed*, **which is that of thought**: **the power to** *disrupt* **and to** *dis-automatize*, **that is,** *to change the rules* —a power that is **knowledge**, which Whitehead, in his " Introductory Summary" to *The Function of Reason*, also called history, and which *is par excellence* the *function* of reason (Whitehead here inherits something from the Kantian framework that I recalled at the beginning of my remarks):

History discloses **two main tendencies** in the course of events. One tendency is exemplified in **the slow decay of physical nature.** With stealthy inevitableness, there is **degradation of energy.** The sources of activity sink downward and downward. Their very matter wastes. **The other tendency is exemplified by the yearly renewal of nature in the spring,** and by the upward course of biological evolution. In these pages, I consider Reason in its relation to these contrasted aspects of history. **Reason is <u>the self-discipline of the originative element</u> in** history. Apart from the operations of Reason, this element is anarchic.①

在怀特海那里，**宇宙学不再是一个领域的问题，而是一个过程的问题**，更准确地说，是一个被速度体系所物化的动态的交互螺旋的问题——其中存在一种作为*无限速度*（*infinite speed*）的东西，即思想的无限速度：**它就是*引起中断、去自动化和改变规则的力量***，这种力量就是*知识*。在怀特海的《理性的功能》（*The Function of Reason*）的"导言"中，他也将这种知识称为历史，它是理性的*最典型的功能*（这里，怀特海从我记得在评论开始时提到过的康德式的框架中继承了某种东西）：

> 历史在时间的过程中形成了两种主要的趋势：一种趋势是以物理自然的缓慢衰减为典型。能力的衰退是一种隐性的必然。活动的源泉不断沉降。任何物质都在耗费着。另一种趋势是以自然年复一年地在春天重新复苏为典型，以生物学进化的上升过程为典型。我认为，理性与这些历史的对立方面相联系着。理性是历史中<u>创造性要素的自我约束</u>。在理性的约束之外，这种要素就处于无

---

① Alfred North Whitehead (1929) Introductory Summary. IN: *The Function of Reason*. Princeton: Princeton University Press.

政府状态了。①

This discipline that is reason, the privilege of **noetic beings in Aristotle's sense**, is obviously **a specific negentropic capacity to "realise" an order in struggling against this "anarchic element"**. I myself argue that **such a faculty is neganthropological and constitutes the *neganthropos***

NEGANTHROPOS

that we strive to be in actuality.

在亚里士多德意义上,这种作为理性、作为智性存在之特权的规律显然是一种特殊的负熵能力,能够在与"反常因素"斗争中"实现"一种规则。我认为,这种能力是负人类学的,并构成了那种我们努力实现的负人(*neganthropos*)。

More often, however, **we are entropic, in particular since the advent of consumer capitalism**— this **capacity to**

---

① Alfred North Whitehead (1929) Introductory Summary. in *The Function of Reason*. Princeton: Princeton University Press. 中译本参见 A. N. 怀特海:《教育与科学理性的功能》,黄铭译,大象出版社,2010 年版。——译者注

change the rules that is **neganthropological reason**

NEGANTHROPOLOGICAL REASON

brings with it a danger of **intersystemic conflict** (highlighted by von Bertalanffy in the introduction to his *General System Theory*, and as this theory's justification). **The pharmacological question** is in this way **inscribed at the heart of cosmology and as the "anthropo-technical", bio-spherical and local consequence that follows from the initial combustion and its universal thermodynamic law.**

然而，通常情况下，我们是熵的，特别是自从消费资本主义出现以来——这种可以改变负人类学理性之规则的能力带来了系统间冲突的危险（这以冯·贝塔朗菲［Von Bertalanffy］① 的《一般系统理论》及其理论的正当性为典型代表）。这样，这个药理学问题就被标定在宇宙学的核心位置，并且，它作为一种"人类-技术的"、生物-领域的和地方性的结果是随着原初燃烧及其普遍的热力学规律而产

---

① 路德维希·冯·贝塔朗菲（Ludwig Von Bertalanffy, 1901—1972）：美籍奥地利理论生物学家和哲学家。他从生物学领域出发，涉猎医学、心理学、行为科学、历史学、哲学等诸多学科，以其渊博的知识、浓厚的人文科学修养，创立了20世纪具有深远意义的一般系统论。代表著作：《一般系统年鉴》（1954）、《一般系统论》（1955）等。——译者注

生的。

To **change the rules** is the power **to move faster than the speed of light**, insofar as **the latter has become**, as the speed of digital automata, **the horizon of the calculation and computing industry**: it is **to move** *infinitely* **fast**, to **escape** established circuits regardless of their speed, and to introduce a **bifurcation**—at **the speed of desire**, that is, **of** *idealization*, *through which neganthropy passes onto the plane of consistence*, making the **noetic economy of desire**, the **line of flight of any neganthropology** that can be realised only **organologically**, that is, **pharmacologically**, and this is the stake of what Whitehead called the function of reason.

The function of Reason is to promote **the art of life.**

The **higher forms of life** are actively engaged in **modifying their environment.** In the case of **mankind** this active **attack on the environment** is **the most prominent fact in his existence.**

The primary function of Reason is the direction of the attack on the environment.

We should compare this with Canguilhem of course.

要**改变这种规则**就要拥有**比光速更快**的力量,后者作为数字化自动装置的速度已经进入计算和计算机行业领域:它能做**无限快速运动**,能逃脱已建立了的速度循环,从而引入一种分叉点——欲望的速度即*理想化的速度*,*由此负人*(*neganthropy*)*转向一致性*(*consistence*)*的状态*,从而形成了**智性的欲望经济**。任何负人类学的飞行线都只能在**器官学**意义和**药理学**意义上实现,这就是怀特海所说的理性的功能:

> 理性的功能就是提升生命的技艺。
> 更高的生命形式就是积极地
> 投身于改变生命的环境。
> 对于人类而言,这种对环境的主动作用
> 就是人类生存中的最重要的事实。
> 理性的主要功能就在于指导这种对环境的
> 作用。

当然,我们要将它与康吉莱姆做个比较。

Such a **power**, however, presupposes **knowledge**, knowledge that is always **the knowledge of powerlessness** (and of a "non-knowledge"). The question then arises of **the laws of the universe conceived as** constituting the field of what we call physics, **a body of rules for a game that we cannot change** — but that we can **localize** and, through this localization, which is also an **augmentation**, which we can **interpret**. That is, we can *organize* this **inorganic**, entropic and sidereal play or game, and this is what we do with nanophysics and quantum technology, at the risk of bringing about, in return, dis-organizations, such as via that new toxicity imposed on organisms by the nanometric infidelity of new milieus of life. And this is so only because the **universe is incomplete, unfinished**, as Whitehead claims.

然而，这种**力量**预设了**知识**，知识总是一种无权的知识（和一种"非-**知识**"的知识）。这个问题是由物理学领域的那种**宇宙规律**引起的，**这是我们无法改变的游戏规则**——但是我们可以将其**局部化**（**localize**）。这同时也是一种**扩展**，通过这种局部化，我们就能进行**解释**，即我们可以*组织*这种**无机的**、熵的和恒星的剧本或游戏，这就是我们利用纳米物理学和量子技术所做的事情。反过来，这又带来了去组织化的危机，比如新的生命环境的纳米背叛性使新的毒性强加于有机体之上。之所以会这样，只是因为**宇宙是不完全的、未完成的**，正如怀特海所说的那样。

Given that technics consists above all in the *organization of inorganic matter*, and this was the main topic of *Technics and time, 1*, leading in turn to the *organological reorganization of cerebral organic matter*, which modifies the play of every somatic organ, and thus gives rise to **a new form of life** (that is, **a new form of negentropy**) that is nevertheless also, as technical, **an accelerator of entropy on all cosmic planes** (and it is this two-sidedness that characterizes the *pharmakon*), there remains a **cosmic question of technics**, and of a technical epoch of **a cosmos within which nanophysics amounts to a transformational inscription** (in Jean-Pierre Dupuy's sense when he refers to transformational technologies), at the quantum level, of re-organization, one that operates via the intermediary of the scanning tunneling microscope.

既然技术在**无机物组织**中构成了上述一切——这是《技术与时间·1》所讨论的主题——并引导转向*智性有机物的器官学的再组织*，这就改变了每一个肉体器官的作用，从而带来新的**生命形式**（即一种新**的负熵形式**）。尽管这也是**熵在所有宇宙领域中的技术性的加速器**（这就是*药*的两面性），但仍然存在一个**宇宙性的技术问题**，一个宇宙的技术时代的问题，其中**纳米物理学**成为一种在量子层面上**转**

型性的再-组织的标定（这是在让-皮埃尔·迪普伊［Jean-Pierre Dupuy］① 所指认的转型性技术的意义上而言的），而这种再-组织是通过扫描穿隧显微镜的中介而实现的。

The **scanning tunneling microscope** is itself a computer capable of **simulating**，that is，of **schematizing**. This **arrangement between the cerebral organ and the quantum scale of hyper-matter** is **a stage of concrescence** that is also a **process of concretization in the broader Simondonian sense** —in that **it operates on all planes of the cosmos at the same time**：**sidereal，vital and psychosocial**，that is，**technical**. This localization can **act retroactively on the play of the whole biosphere**，into which it can in a way spread itself generally（through a process of **amplification**②），and **this has now engendered that specific stage of concrescence that we refer to in our epoch as the Anthropocene**.

这种**扫描穿隧显微镜**是一种能**模拟**和**按计划运行**的计算机。这种**在智性器官和超物质的量子范围内的安排**是一

---

① 让-皮埃尔·迪普伊（Jean-Pierre Dupuy，1941— ）：法国工程师、哲学家。法国巴黎综合理工学院社会政治哲学教授、美国斯坦福大学政治学教授。其代表作有：《自我欺骗与合理性悖论》（1998）、《思想的机械化：认知科学的起源》（2000）等。——译者注

② See Gilbert Simondon（2010）*Communication et information*：*Cours et conférences*. Chatou：Les Editions de la Transparence.

个共生的阶段,也是一种在更广义的西蒙栋意义上的具体化过程——它同时在宇宙的各个领域运行着:恒星领域、生命领域和社会心理领域即技术领域。这种地方化能够反过来对整个生物圈产生影响,从而在某种意义上普遍地(通过一种放大[amplification]过程①)传播自身,而这已经在我们所说的人类纪时代中产生了特殊的共生阶段。

Technics obviously **respects the laws of physics**, since otherwise it would not function. But **technics, as "matter that functions" organologically (and constituting as such what I propose calling hyper-matter), locally trans-forms the cosmic order in ways that are not predictable**. Hence the **concretization of the technical individual** as a mode of existence, the functioning of which cannot **be dissolved into the laws of physics**, tends to give rise to **associated techno-geographical milieus**.

显然,技术尊重物理规律,否则它就无法发挥功能。但是,技术作为器官学意义上的"功能物"(构成了我所说的超物质),以不可预知的方式局部地改变着宇宙规则。因此,技术个人的具体化(concretization of the technical

---

① 同上。

individual）作为一种存在方式，它的功能不能被融入物理规律，而是趋向于产生**联合的技术-地理学的环境**（**associated techno-geographical milieus**）。

It was for this reason that Simondon claimed the need for a **mechanology** that I prefer to understand as an **organology**, given that mechanology does not enable us **to think pharmacologically,** or to think **the links between psychic, technical and collective individuation.**

因此，西蒙栋认为需要**机械学**（**mechanology**），而我更愿意将其理解为**器官学**，因为机械学不能使我们在**药理学**意义上进行思考，或者**不能思考心理个体化、技术个体化和集体个体化之间的联系**。

Processes, concrescence, disruptions, infidelities of milieus, and metastable equilibriums (and thus disequilibriums) all form what, in our epoch, presents itself to us as **what we are causing** *within* **ourselves,** *around* **us,** and *between* **us,** as projections of a becoming that we are no longer able to trans-form into a future on the basis of our **organological and pharmacological condition,** that is, as the **play between the processes of psychic, technical and collective** (**that is**, **social**) **individuation**, processes through which and in which we always find ourselves tied to these three dimensions by their mutual organological condition.

在我们时代中所有形式的过程、共生、中断、环境的背叛、亚稳定平衡（及非平衡），都向我们展现为*在我们自身*、*在我们周围*以及*在我们之间*所引起的东西，即一种生成的投射。在这种生成中，我们不再能够基于我们的器官学和药理学的条件转向一种未来，这种条件就是心理个体化、技术个体化和集体（社会）个体化过程之间的游戏。通过这些过程，并在这些过程中，我们总能发现自己是凭借这三种相互作用的器官学条件而与它们紧密联系着。

It seems **today that this play and this game is turning into a massacre**, wherein psychic and collective individuation are being killed off by a technical individuation that is slave to a self-destructive economy, because it is **destructive of the social milieus without which no technical milieu is possible that does not at the same time destroy the physical milieus of the biosphere**.

今天，这种游戏似乎变为一种屠杀，其中心理的和集体的个体化被技术的个体化所扼杀，而后者又被自我毁灭的经济所奴役，因为**没有这种社会环境的破坏性，技术环境就不可能存在，但这种社会环境的破坏性并不同时破坏生物圈中的物理环境**。

The *general ecological* question **poses and imposes on this tripartite division the question of biological, geographical and cosmic systems and processes**, such that they thoroughly infuse, constantly, locally, and **in conditions of locality that remain totally to be thought**, the processes of psychic, technical and social individuation. In addition to analysing the condition of transindividuation through co-individuation of the processes of psychic, technical and social individuation, **general organology studies the conditions of returning to vital biological sources, and of doing so in the cosmic, entropic and sidereal conditions of negentropy, insofar as these are made possible by scientific and noetic instruments.**

*一般生态学*问题可以分为三个维度，即生物学的问题、地理学的问题以及宇宙的系统与过程的问题。因此，他们**在仍需要被整体思考的地方性条件下**，彻底地、持续地和具体地影响着心理的、技术的和社会的个体化过程。除了分析通过在心理的、技术的和社会的个体化过程中的共同个体化而进行的超个体化状况，**一般器官学还研究了回归**

重要生物资源的条件,以及在宇宙的、熵的和恒星的负熵条件下这样做的条件,而这需要借助科学和智性的仪器才有可能。

Through this dual approach, general organology investigates the conditions of possibility of a political and noetic *decision*, a decision that is made possible by grammatization. And at the same time it investigates **the specific regime of the *pharmakon* that is established by grammatization, which is haunted by the question of proletarianization.** The realities of the latter, in terms of subsistence and existence, must be studied for each epoch of the **"history of the supplement"**, given that, failing the development of therapies and therapeutics, **proletarianization has the effect of eliminating the possibility of decision, that is, of neganthropogenesis.**

Translated by Daniel Ross

一般器官学通过这种双重路径来研究一种政治的和智性的*决断*的可能性条件,而这种决断借助编程化才成为可能。同时,一般器官学也研究**由编程化建立的*药*的特殊方法,但这又受到无产阶级化问题的困扰。**鉴于治疗和治疗学没有发展,而无产阶级化已经造成减少决断的可能性,即负人类生成的可能性的效果。因此，从生计（subsistence）和生存（existence）的角度来看，无产阶级化的现实必须作为每个时代的"**替补的历史（history of the supplement）**"来加以研究。

本文的英文版由 Daniel Ross 翻译

EIGHTH COURSE
13 APRIL 2016
/
Reading Marx in the Anthropocene
From the German Ideology to Das Kapital

第 八 讲
2016.4.13
在人类纪阅读马克思：
从《德意志意识形态》到《资本论》

Last week I tried to show you why and how Marx misinterpreted the famous dialectic of the master and the slave, and why this one is not a slave: since he is a knecht, that is, a servant.

上周，我已经设法向你们说明了马克思是为什么和如何误读了著名的主-奴辩证法，以及为什么这个奴隶不再是奴隶：因为他是一个雇工（knecht），即一个仆人（servant）。

*

Another question is the fact that Marx doesn't question the ambiguous status of technology as it is a *pharmakon*—and this is one of the reasons for which Marxism is so often considered to be a determinism.

另一个问题则涉及这样一个事实,即马克思没有对技术的含糊地位提出质疑,也没有将技术看作一种*药*——这也是为什么马克思主义往往被看作一种决定论的原因之一。

I wanted to show you today what are the systemic limits of capitalism today as Anthropocene, but we don't have time and since you have the text which addresses this question, I prefer to let you read it. So I will finish this seminar by proposing comments of the *Grundrisse*.

我原本想在今天给你们阐述一下现在处于人类纪的资本主义的系统性界限。但由于我们的时间有限,而且你们已经有了说明这一问题的文本,因此我更乐意让你们自己去阅读它。所以,我将通过尝试性地对《大纲》做些评论来结束这次研讨课程。

*

By failing to pose either the question of the *toxicity* of the *pharmakon*, or that of its *curativity* and the therapeutic this presupposes (which is always a system of de-proletarianization), the Marxist *negative* dialectic leads to the doctrine of the dictatorship of the proletariat, and not to a political project of de-proletarianization, that is, to a reacquisition of knowledge in the service of the individuation of citizens.

由于既没有提出药的*毒性*问题，也没有提出药的*治愈性*问题及其预想的治疗方法（它始终是一种去无产阶级化的体系），因此，马克思主义的否定辩证法产生了无产阶级专政的学说，而不是一种去无产阶级化的政治方案，即在市民的个体化中重新获得知识。

This outcome was due not to Marx being wrong, but because philosophy is collective work, and those who contribute to its individuation are able to do so *only in their time* —and *as* their time becomes *the time of everyone*.

这种结果不是因为马克思错了，而是因为哲学是一种集体事业。人们只能为其所处时代的个体化做出贡献——因为他们的时代变成了*每个人的时代*。

Marx, of course, could not conceive all this and the way that it could and should come to modify his own concepts. Because these concepts were unavailable to him, and because exteriorisation itself had not yet reached the stage that would require thinking grammatization as such (as the pharmacological spatialization of time in the form of tertiary retention), Marx was not able to pose the question of a curative pharmacology, that is, a positive pharmacology.

马克思，当然做不到考虑所有时代，也无法再更改他自己的思想。因为这些概念对他来说还是难以获得的，因为外化（exteriorization）本身还没有达到一个需要思考编程化的阶段（比如，在第三持存形式中时间的药理学的空间化），所以，马克思没能提出治疗的药理学即积极的药理学的问题。

The failure of poststructuralism to pose this question seems to lie, rather, more in the fact that it ignores the scope of the Marxist understanding of technics, despite the analyses of Kostas Axelos. But for Marx, he would not have been in a position to envisage this curativity as techno-logical and industrial individuation, reconstituting knowledge and participating in the struggle against proletarianization.

后结构主义在这一问题上的失败似乎主要在于它忽视了马克思主义的技术理解视域，尽管科斯塔斯·亚克色罗斯(Kostas Axelos)① 曾做过分析。但对马克思来说,他还没有能够将这种治疗设想为一种可以重建知识或者反对无产阶级化的技术的和工业的个体化。

This *dialectic of work and workers*, which is obviously the foundation of Marxism, in Hegel describes less the situation of the *worker becoming proletarian* than that of the *artisan becoming an entrepreneur*, that is, bourgeois. In other words, *the reappropriation of this dialectic by Marxism is based on a misunderstanding.*

显然,构成马克思主义之基础的工作和工人的辩证法,在黑格尔那里,并不是工人变成无产者的情况,而是工匠(artisan)变为企业家(entrepreneur)即资产者的情况。换句话说,马克思主义对这种辩证法的挪用是基于一种误解之上的。

What Hegel nevertheless does not think here—where he analyses the *becoming of objective spirit by and in work*, and as a stage of the "work of the concept"—is the

---

① 科斯塔斯·亚克色罗斯（Kostas Axelos, 1924—2010）：希腊-法国哲学家，西方马克思主义理论家，自称开放的马克思主义者。曾是希腊共产党员(1941—1945)，后被驱逐出党，于1945年流亡法国。其代表作有：《马克思思想中的异化、实践和技术》(1976) 等。——译者注

machine's work, which deprives the worker of his singularity, that is, of his work, which becomes a job (a salary), a *negativity* that turns it into a pure *force* of labour that is no longer work properly speaking, given that work, as Hegel explains here, is an individuation process in which the worker is individuated at the same time as the object, which thus individuates itself technically (this is what I have tried to describe as work in an associated milieu).

而黑格尔没有思考的东西——在他对*绝对精神通过工作并在工作中的生成*即"概念运作"一个阶段的分析中——是*机器*的工作，它剥夺了工人的独特性和工作（work），工作（work）变成了职业（job）（工资），这种*否定性*将工人变为纯粹的劳动力，这种劳动不再是工作，因为正如黑格尔所说的，工作是一种个体化过程，在这个过程中，工人同时被个体化为对象，即在技术上将自身个体化（这就是我试图描述的在一种联合的环境中的工作）。

This is why, inasmuch as the essence of Marxist economico-political theory will turn out to be a **dictatorship of the proletariat** supposedly grounded in this dialectic, it is based on **a profound misinterpretation.** For **Marx himself showed in the *Grundrisse* that the determination carried out by** exteriorisation *in machines*, and as *grammatization*, is *what structurally and materially deprives the slave of all knowledge* —the slave who becomes the worker, the wage labourer, **a status destined to be extended to "all layers of the population"** via wage labour, as Marx and Engels write in the *Communist Manifesto*.①

就马克思主义的经济-政治理论的本质将会导致基于这个辩证法假设上的**无产阶级专政**来说,这就是为什么说它是建立在**一种深刻的误读**基础之上的原因。因为**马克思自己在《大纲》中就表明,在机器中由外化所执行的规则,作为编程化,就是结构性地、物质性地剥夺奴隶的所有知识的东西**——这就变成了奴隶,即工人、雇佣劳动者,这种身份注定会通过雇佣劳动的方式**被扩展到"所有阶层的人们"**,正如马克思和恩格斯在《共产党宣言》②中所写的那样。

*

In *Das Kapital*, Marx's gesture consists, on the one

---

① Karl Marx and Friedrich Engels, *The Communist Manifesto*, p. 88, translation modified.
② 同上。参见《马克思恩格斯文集》第 2 卷,人民出版社,2009 年版,第 38—39 页。——译者注

hand, *in making the concept of the proletariat synonymous with the concept of the working class*, and, on the other hand, *in taking* **the negativity of the proletarian condition** *as an* **unsurpassable horizon** *and in* **never posing the question or the hypothesis of de-proletarianization**—a **Marxist leaning** that prolongs **Hegelian metaphysics.**

在《资本论》中，马克思一方面*使无产阶级概念与工人阶级概念具有相同含义*，另一方面*将无产阶级状况的否定性看作一种无法超越的界限，从来没有提出去无产阶级化的问题或假设*，即一种延续了黑格尔式的形而上学的马克思主义倾向。

Now, we know that free software organization of work, for example, is based on de-proletarianization, itself being based on the controbutivity made possible by the contributive technologies that appeared with the net and especially the web, for example, Wikipedia.

现在，我们知道，提供免费软件的工作组织是建立在去无产阶级化基础之上的，而去无产阶级化本身是基于贡献性之上的，这种贡献性是随着网络（net）尤其是网站——比如维基百科——而使贡献性技术而成为可能的。

In other words, Marxian philosophy is not capable here to anticipate the evolution of technology as it is the one of digital tertiary retention.

换言之，马克思哲学在这一点上没有能够预见技术的进化，即作为数字第三持存的技术进化。

What Hegel doesn't think is *technics as that which bypasses and short-circuits the knowledge of the worker thus becoming a slave, no longer a knecht, no longer serving the master directly, but the machinery.* To the contrary, **Marx attempts to think** *machine technology***, but he does so** <u>*without drawing any consequences for the master-knecht dialectic*</u>. Because **he "forgets" to think the positive and negative pharmacology of the organology** that is constituted by the process of exosomatisation, he **turns the** *negativity of the universal subject* **of** history (**that would be the proletariat**) **into the** *revolutionary principle*, whereas **it is the** <u>*curative positivity of the pharmacological supplement deriving from work that inverts the logic of disindividuation*</u>, and **as technique** *of the self*, and that must *make possible* **a new age of individuation, that is,** *of knowledge.* And it must do so as **a new history of the love of knowledge**, its savours, as **savoir-faire**

and as **savoir-vivre** as well as **theoretical knowledge**.

黑格尔没有考虑到的是，*技术会使工人的知识发生短路和绕避，因而工人就变为一个奴隶，而不再是一个雇工，不再直接服务于主人，而是直接服务于机器*。相反，马克思试图思考机器技术，但是他这样做时并没有对主-奴辩证法做出任何的推进。因为，他"忘记"了思考由外在化过程所构成的*器官学*的积极和消极的药理学，而是将普遍的历史主体（无产阶级）的否定性变为革命的原则。然而，*正是从工作中产生的药理学替补的治疗积极性将非个体化的逻辑颠倒过来*，并使其颠倒为*自主的技艺*（technique of the self），从而必然使*个体化即知识的新阶段*成为可能。这一定是作为*热爱知识*（技能知识、生活知识和理论知识）*的新历史阶段*而展开的。

Marx described the **process of proletarianization** in the *Communist Manifesto* (1848), and he described it **as the loss of knowledge resulting from exteriorisation**, a viewpoint that would be **further developed in the** *Grundrisse* (1857).

马克思在《*共产党宣言*》(1848) 中描述了*无产阶级化的过程*，将其描述*由于外化而导致的知识的丧失*，这个观点*在《大纲》*(1857) *中被进一步发展了*。

The proletariat *is not* **the working class, but the** *non-working* **class** [*la classe des désoeuvres*]**,** that is, the downgraded, the class of those who are *de-class-ified*. **They are those who** *no longer know*, **but** *serve without knowledge*, **because they serve not a master, but systems that exteriorize knowledge** EVEN FOR THE "MASTERS".

无产阶级不是工人阶级，而是非-工人阶级（*non-working* class [*la classe des désoeuvres*]），即衰落了的、去阶级化了的（*de-class-ified*）人所构成的阶级。他们是那些一无所知的、不以知识提供服务的人，因为他们服侍的不是主人，而是服侍把知识外化给"主人"的体系。

*

The Hegelian and "idealist" definition of the *understanding* was **inverted by Marx when he proposed that exteriorisation, in which understanding essentially consists, is first and foremost that of the means of production**: such is his "materialism". But in so dismissing idealism **Marx lost sight of the question of ideality, that is, idealization as what is at work in all investment and in all knowledge of the object of desire**.

当马克思提出外化（exteriorisation）——知性在本质上就在于外化——首先且最重要的是生产手段即他的"唯物主义"时，对*知性*（understanding）的黑格尔式的、"唯心主义"的定义就被马克思所颠倒了。但是，在这种对唯心主义的清算中，马克思忽视了理想（ideality）问题，即在欲望对象的一切投入和一切知识中运作的理想化。

And **poststructuralism**, too, leaves this in the shadows, tending as it does to **confuse desire and drive**: *the misunderstanding in relation to the proletariat is at the same time a misunderstanding of desire.*

后结构主义也遮蔽了这一问题，并**混淆了欲望**（desire）**和驱力**（drive）：这种关于无产阶级的误解同时也是对欲望的误解。

In **The German Ideology** (1845), Marx's materialism consists *firstly* in **identifying the first "historical act" of noetic beings with their technical capacity**. Non-inhuman beings

begin to distinguish themselves from animals as soon as they begin to *produce* their means of subsistence, a step which is conditioned by their physical organisation.

在《德意志意识形态》(1845) 中，马克思的唯物主义首先在于确认智性存在运用他们的技术能力所进行的第一个"历史活动"。非-非人存在（Non-inhuman beings）即，

> 一旦人开始生产自己的生活资料，即迈出由他们的肉体组织所决定的这一步的时候，人本身就开始把自己和动物区别开来。①

The **Hegelian question of exteriorisation** is thus "**put back on its feet**", in some way **as a question of general organology**, where **the materialist dialectic assigns** *being*（**and its becoming**）**to** *doing*, **that is, to** *production*.

As individuals express their life, so they are. What they are, therefore, coincides with their production, both with *what* they produce and with *how* they produce. Hence what individuals are depends on the material conditions of

---

① 参见《马克思恩格斯文集》第 1 卷，人民出版社，2009 年版，第 519 页。——译者注

their production.

这样，黑格尔式的外化问题就"重新回到原点"，在某种程度上成为一个一般器官学的问题，这里，唯物辩证法将存在（及其生成）指定为行动（*doing*），即生产：

> 他们是什么样的，这同他们的生产是一致的——既和他们生产什么一致，又和他们怎样生产一致。因而，个人是什么样的，这取决于他们进行生产的物质条件。①

We already saw that this the definition of being as pro-duction and re-pro-duction, that is, as exo-somatisation based on a process of artificial selection.

我们已经将存在定义为生产和再生产，即基于人为选择的标准化过程的外在化（exo-somatisation）。

That **this exteriorisation can lead to the proletarianization of workers** is explained in the *Grundrisse* in terms of the ***passage from the tool to the machine***, that is, ***to a new stage of***

---

① 参见《马克思恩格斯文集》第 1 卷，人民出版社，2009 年版，第 520 页。——译者注

exteriorisation.

The means of labour passes through different metamorphoses, whose culmination is the *machine*, or rather, **an *automatic system of machinery*** (system of machinery: the *automatic* one is merely its most complete, most adequate form, and alone transforms machinery into a system) [⋯]; **this automaton consisting of numerous mechanical and intellectual organs, so that the workers themselves are cast merely as its conscious linkages.**①

这种能够导致工人的无产阶级化的外化在《大纲》中是根据**从工具到机器，即一个外化的新阶段的变迁**来加以解释的：

劳动资料经历了各种不同的形态变化，它的最后的形态是机器，或者更确切些说，是*自动的机器体系*(即机器体系：自动的机器体系不过是最完善、最适当的机器体系形式，只有它才使机器成为体系)……这种自动机是由许多机械器官和

---

① Karl Marx. *Grundrisse*, p. 692.

智能器官组成的，因此，工人自己只是被当作自动的机器体系的有意识的肢体。①

Here, the labourers are not still workers, because a worker works, this meaning, opens a world, in french, œuvre. Those labourers have become themselves organs of this machinery, exactly like a software or a horse or a slave that is not at all, here, precisely, a knecht.

这里，劳动者仍然不是工人，因为一个工人在工作意味着他打开了一个世界，用法语说就是"œuvre"。而那些劳动者已经变成机器的器官，就像一个软件或一匹马，或者一个奴隶（slave），准确地说是一个雇工（knecht）。

And Marx continues,

In no way does the machine appear as the individual worker's means of labour. Its distinguishing characteristic is not in the least, as with the means of labour, **to transmit the worker's activity to the object; this activity**, rather, **is posited in such a way**

---

① 同上。参见《马克思恩格斯全集》第31卷，人民出版社，1998年版，第90页。——译者注

that it merely transmits the machine's work, the machine's action, on to the raw material — supervises it and guards against interruptions. **Not as with the instrument**, which the worker animates and makes into his organ with his skill and strength, and **whose handling** therefore **depends on his virtuosity**. Rather, **it is the machine which possesses skill and strength in place of the worker, is itself the virtuoso, with a soul of its own in the mechanical laws acting through it.**①

马克思继续说：

　　机器无论在哪一方面都不表现为单个工人的劳动资料。机器的特征绝不是像［单个工人的］劳动资料那样，在工人的活动作用于［劳动］对象方面起中介作用；相反地，<u>工人的活动表现为：它只是在机器的运转，机器作用于原材料方面起中介作用</u>——看管机器，防止它发生故障，这和对待工具的情形不一样。工人把工具当作器官，通过自己的技能和活动赋予它以灵魂，因此，掌

---

① Karl Marx. *Grundrisse*, pp. 692 - 693.

握工具的能力取决于工人的技艺。相反，**机器则代替工人而具有技能和力量，它本身就是能工巧匠，它通过在自身中发生作用的力学规律而具有自己的灵魂**。①

This analysis forms the basis of **Simondon's argument in** ***Du mode d'existence des objets techniques***. The process of **disindividuation** that he describes paraphrases these statements by Marx.

The **technical individual** becomes at a certain point **man's adversary**, **his competitor**, because **man had, when there were only tools, centralized all technical individuality** within himself; **the machine then takes the place of man** because man gives to the machine **the function of tool-bearer**.②

这种分析形成了**西蒙栋在《技术客体的存在方式》**（***Du mode d'existence des objets techniques***）中的观点的基础，他对**去个体化**过程的描述就是基于对马克思的阐述：

---

① 同上。参见《马克思恩格斯全集》第31卷，人民出版社，1998年版，第90—91页。——译者注
② Gilbert Simondon, *Du mode d'existence des objets techniques*, p. 15.

技术个体在某个点上变成了人的对手,竞争者,因为曾经只有工具的人,现在已经集中了所有的技术个体于自身;然后,机器取代了人的位置,因为人给了机器关涉工具的功能。①

Marx does indeed emphasize that this industrial division of labour, and **the replacement of workers and tools by machines, is** also **a change in the status of knowledge and of the science that it brings.** Scientific knowledge is **placed at the service of the process of exteriorisation**, whereby knowledge itself, and in general, is that which exteriorizes itself. And this exteriorisation is the new regime of exosomatisation that characterize our times as **disruption**, that **short-circuits and by-passes social systems**—but this consequences are self-destructive, and here we can see why we need to reinterpreted Marx and Engels's philosophy as well as to reconsider what is politics faced with digital economy.

马克思确实强调了工业的劳动分工、**机器对工人和工具的取代**,由此也带来了知识和科学的地位变化。科学知识被置于服务外化过程的位置,由此,知识自身(知识一

---

① 同上。

般）也外化了自身。而这种外化（exteriorisation）正是新的外在化（exosomatisation）的制度，后者使我们的时代表现为**中断，使社会体系发生短路和绕道**——但是，这个结果是自我毁灭的，这里我们就知道我们为什么需要重新解读马克思和恩格斯的哲学，以及重新思考面对数字化经济的政治学是什么。

This seminar is now finished, and next year, we will try to go deepen in the question of truth, knowledge, capitalism and digital technologies in the Anthropocene.

到这里，我们的研讨课就结束了。明年，我们将尝试对人类纪中的真理、知识、资本主义和数字技术（digital technologies）问题进行深入探讨。

图书在版编目(CIP)数据

南京课程:在人类纪时代阅读马克思和恩格斯:从
《德意志意识形态》到《自然辩证法》:汉英对照／
(法)贝尔纳・斯蒂格勒著;张福公译. —南京:南京
大学出版社,2019.10(2021.1 重印)
(当代激进思想家译丛/张一兵主编)
ISBN 978-7-305-19852-6

Ⅰ.①南… Ⅱ.①贝… ②张… Ⅲ.①马克思主义哲
学—研究—汉、英 Ⅳ.①B0-0

中国版本图书馆 CIP 数据核字(2018)第 012746 号

From *German Ideology* to the *Dialectics of Nature*
Copyright © 2018 By Bernard Stiegler
Simplified Chinese translation copyright © 2019 by Nanjing University Press

江苏省版权局著作权合同登记 图字:10-2019-277 号

出 版 者	南京大学出版社		
社 址	南京市汉口路 22 号	邮 编	210093
出 版 人	金鑫荣		

丛 书 名 当代激进思想家译丛
书   名 南京课程:在人类纪时代阅读马克思和恩格斯
　　　　　——从《德意志意识形态》到《自然辩证法》
著   者 [法]贝尔纳・斯蒂格勒
译   者 张福公
责任编辑 洪 洋　张 静
照   排 南京紫藤制版印务中心
印   刷 江苏苏中印刷有限公司
开   本 920×1194　1/32　印张 9.5　字数 185 千
版   次 2019 年 10 月第 1 版　2021 年 1 月第 2 次印刷
ISBN 978-7-305-19852-6
定   价 69.00 元

网　　　址:http://www.njupco.com
官方微博:http://weibo.com/njupco
官方微信:njupress
销售咨询热线:(025)83594756

＊ 版权所有,侵权必究
＊ 凡购买南大版图书,如有印装质量问题,请与所购
  图书销售部门联系调换